MY BIG BIG BOOK OF

ANIMALS

This a Parragon Book

First Published in 2001 Parragon, Queen Street House, 4 Queen Street, Bath BA1 1HE, UK

Copyright © Parragon 2001

ISBN 0-75256-301-7

Produced by **ticktock** *Publishing Ltd.*

Illustrations by John Alston

Photography by Roddy Paine Studios

Additional pictures supplied by: FLPA 14/15main, 38/39main, 39cr, 42/43main, 49cr, 59c, 65cr, 78cl, 84cr, 88cr, 96/97main, 96l, 100r, 106main, 107r, 113cr. Planet Earth 36r, 43r, 48c, 83r, 89main, 98/99main, 99r, 102t, 105main, 104l. Heather Angel 104r, 121c. Oxford Scientific Pictures 83r, 100/101main.

Printed in China

MY BIG BIG BOOK OF
ANIMALS

BY BARBARA TAYLOR

p

CONTENTS

This is a book all about animals – farm animals, pets, birds, animals that live in the ocean and those that live in the rainforest. There are scaly reptiles, creepy crawlies, and some very, very dangerous animals indeed!

Keeping pets is a great way of learning about animals. As you play with them, cuddle them, and look after them, your pets will become your special friends. Don't forget that pets depend on people to care for them every day of their lives. Some pets, such as cats, dogs and ponies, live for a very long time!

FARM

From cows and sheep to pigs and goats, we keep all sorts of animals on our farms. They provide us with food to eat and materials, such as wool and leather, to make clothes and shoes. Farmers have to know a lot about their animals in order to look after them. Some animals, such as sheepdogs, help farmers with their work.

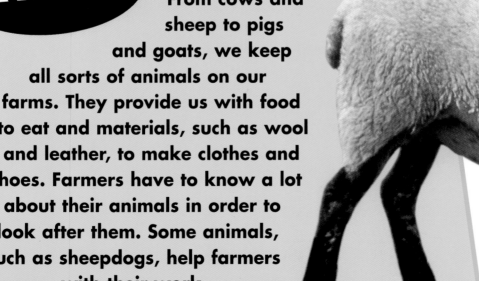

 **M**eet seven animals in each section and learn amazing facts as well as essential information about each one. Then turn to pages 122-125 to have fun in the Big, Big Animal Quiz.

JUNGLE

Rainforests are full of animals because they are warm places with plenty of food, water and places to hide and nest. Birds and bats fly through the treetops, while monkeys leap from branch to branch. Animals such as tree frogs have special ways of clinging to slippery leaves and twigs. The forest floor is home to big and spectacular animals such as tigers, elephants and gorillas.

OCEAN

Oceans cover over 70 per cent of the world. They teem with life, from coral reefs and sunny coastlines, to the mysterious ocean depths. Fishes such as sharks and mackerel are speedy swimmers but other sea animals, such as crabs, creep along much more slowly. Mammals such as dolphins and sea lions live in the oceans too, but have to come to the surface to breathe air.

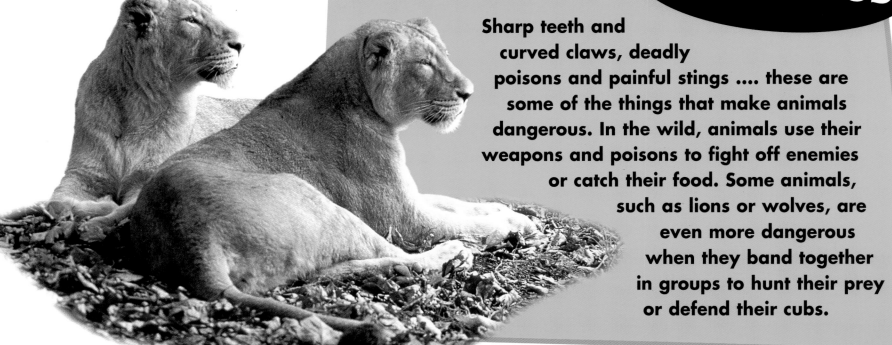

Sharp teeth and curved claws, deadly poisons and painful stings .... these are some of the things that make animals dangerous. In the wild, animals use their weapons and poisons to fight off enemies or catch their food. Some animals, such as lions or wolves, are even more dangerous when they band together in groups to hunt their prey or defend their cubs.

REPTILES

Reptiles are animals such as tortoises and turtles, snakes and lizards, crocodiles and alligators. They have dry, scaly, waterproof skins and most of them live in warm places on land. Their bodies are the same temperature as their surroundings. Most reptiles lay eggs with soft, leathery shells and do not look after their young.

BIRDS

Birds are the only animals with feathers. Some, such as peacocks, have amazingly colourful feathers. Others, such as owls, have camouflaged feathers. Most birds can fly, but a few birds, such as penguins and ostriches, cannot fly at all. Birds lay eggs with a hard shell and most birds build nests to keep their eggs and young safe and warm.

CREEPY CRAWLIES

Creepy crawlies are animals such as scary spiders, slimy snails, beautiful butterflies and squiggly worms. Insects, such as butterflies, have six legs, spiders have eight legs, snails have one big foot and worms have no legs at all. Most insects have wings and can fly, but creepy crawlies such as worms and snails creep and crawl along at very slow speeds.

JELLY BABIES

When hamsters are born, they have no fur and look like tiny pink jelly baby sweets. Their mother may tuck them inside her cheek pouches if she senses danger. Baby hamsters start to grow their fur when they are about a week old.

A HAMSTER'S FACE LOOKS VERY FAT WHEN ITS CHEEK POUCHES ARE STUFFED FULL OF FOOD.

THEY HAVE VERY POOR EYESIGHT.

THEY HAVE SHARP FRONT TEETH FOR GNAWING THINGS.

A HAMSTER CAN HAVE A BABY WHEN IT IS ONLY 16 DAYS OLD.

HAMSTER

Hamsters are clean, friendly, busy little animals that usually sleep in the day and wake up at night. They have short tails and cheek pouches in which they carry food. They only live for two or three years, but make nice little pets.

HOME SWEET HOME

Make sure you shut the door to your hamster's cage properly because they are very good at escaping! Give your hamster plenty of food and water every day and clean the cage out at least once a week. A solid wheel in the cage or a plastic ball that rolls around the floor helps your hamster to get the exercise it needs to stay fit and healthy.

FINGER PUPPET

Hamsters will soon become tame if you are gentle and patient and play with them every day. They may bite but only if they are frightened or startled.

DOG

Pet dogs love to be with people and are loyal and faithful friends if they are trained well. Some are so well trained they can guide visually impaired people in their daily lives. Dogs treat their owners as the leader of their pack.

DROOPY EARS

A spaniel's ears are hairy and hang down by the sides of its head. Dogs with floppy ears cannot hear as well as dogs with ears that stand up straight.

LET'S PLAY BALL!

Dogs love to play games, such as chasing after balls and sticks, finding toys that you have hidden or playing tug of war. Make sure balls are big enough so your dog can't swallow them and choke. Choose sticks that do not have sharp bits or nails sticking out.

DOGS' TAILS WAG WHEN THEY ARE HAPPY OR EXCITED.

PUPPY PROGRESS

When puppies are born, they are blind and deaf. They do not begin to see and hear until they are about eight days old. By the time they are three weeks old, puppies can walk and start to explore.

DOGS MOULT THEIR FUR SO THEY HAVE A THIN SUMMER COAT AND A THICK WINTER COAT.

LARGE EYES FACE FORWARDS SO DOGS CAN SEE IN 3D.

A LONG, WET NOSE GIVES A DOG A GOOD SENSE OF SMELL.

LONG LEGS HELP THEM TO RUN FAST FOR LONG DISTANCES.

DOGS CANNOT PULL IN THEIR CLAWS LIKE CATS.

DID YOU KNOW?

A dog's sense of smell is about one million times more sensitive than yours and it can hear many sounds that you cannot hear.

PET DOGS ARE RELATED TO WILD WOLVES!

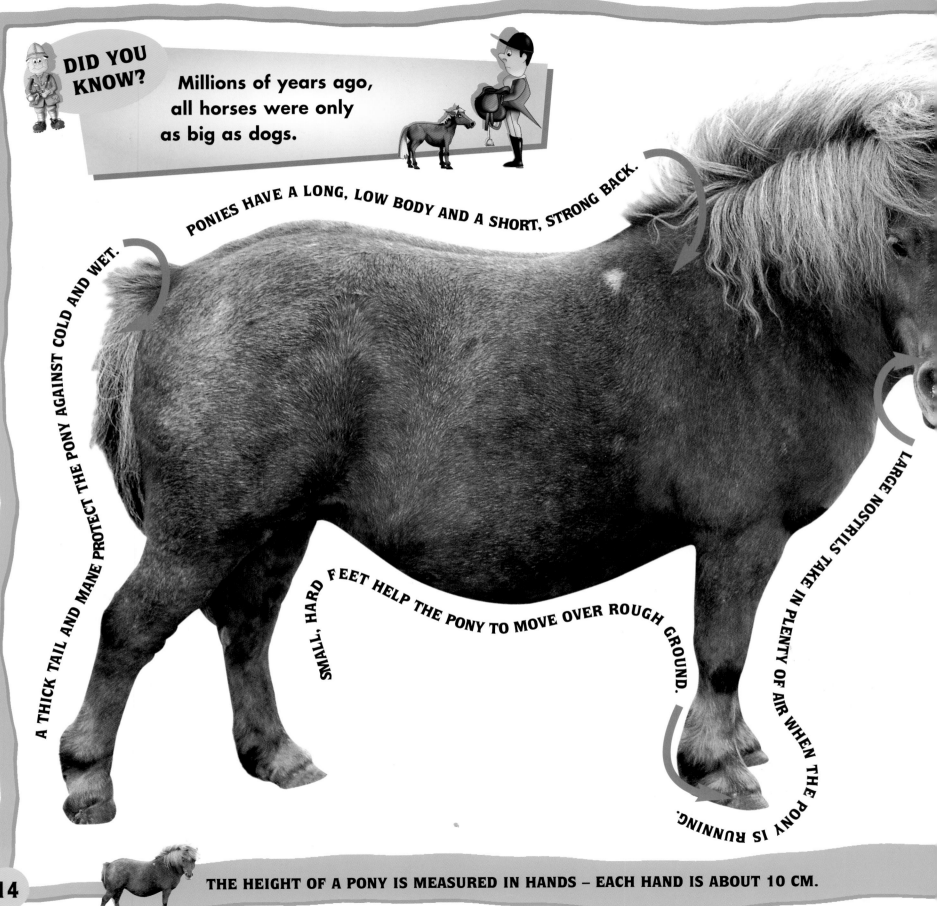

PONIES HAVE A LONG, LOW BODY AND A SHORT, STRONG BACK.

A THICK TAIL AND MANE PROTECT THE PONY AGAINST COLD AND WET.

SMALL, HARD FEET HELP THE PONY TO MOVE OVER ROUGH GROUND.

LARGE NOSTRILS TAKE IN PLENTY OF AIR WHEN THE PONY IS RUNNING.

THE HEIGHT OF A PONY IS MEASURED IN HANDS – EACH HAND IS ABOUT 10 CM.

PONY

Ponies are hardy, small horses less than 1.47 metres high. Most ponies are friendly if you treat them kindly. They enjoy being made a fuss of and soon learn to recognise you as a friend.

EAR TALK

A pony's ears are always twitching, listening to sounds in front and behind. If a pony is cross, both its ears lie flat and the whites of its eyes show. If the ears are forward, it shows that a pony is listening and interested.

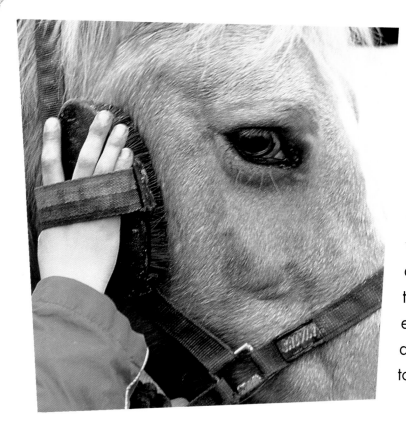

WASH AND BRUSH UP

Grooming a pony helps to keep its skin clean and healthy and its coat glossy. Ponies are groomed when their coat is dry because it's easier to brush. Most ponies enjoy being groomed and may even nod off to sleep!

ON THE HOOF

Metal horseshoes nailed to a pony's hoof protect the hoof and help the pony to grip the ground. A pony's hooves are very strong because they have to take the weight of the whole body.

A PONY'S HOOF IS MADE FROM THE SAME STUFF AS YOUR FINGERNAILS.

GUINEA PIG

Guinea pigs are timid, gentle pets that are easy to hold and tame. They come in many different colours and their fur can be short or long as well as smooth or coarse. They also live in the wild in some countries.

A GUINEA PIG'S COAT CAN BE A MIXTURE OF COLOURS.

DOING YOUR EXERCISES

Guinea pigs are greedy animals and will grow fat if they do not get enough exercise. An exercise pen helps them to stay healthy. It can be moved onto the grass and should have food and water inside.

NOISY PIGS

Guinea pigs are noisy animals. They 'talk' to each other using a variety of chirps, squeaks, whistles or burbles.

FURRY BABIES

When guinea pigs are born, they are covered in fur and their eyes and ears are open. They can run around after about an hour and only suckle their mother's milk for three weeks.

GUINEA PIGS CAN LIVE UP TO 8 YEARS.

THE LARGE, ALERT EYES WATCH FOR DANGER.

DID YOU KNOW?

Wild guinea pigs are called cavies. They live in small family groups in the grasslands of South America.

GUINEA PIGS HAVE STOUT BODIES WITH SHORT LEGS AND NO TAIL.

SHARP CLAWS ARE USED FOR DIGGING.

THEY HAVE STRONG TEETH FOR GNAWING.

ALBINO GUINEA PIGS ARE WHITE WITH PINK EYES.

In Sweden, you can go and see rabbit show-jumping!

BIG EYES WATCH FOR DANGER.

LONG BACK LEGS HELP IT TO HOP FAST.

A TWITCHING NOSE THAT HAS A GOOD SENSE OF SMELL.

RABBITS HAVE FUR UNDER THEIR FEET FOR A GOOD GRIP.

THERE ARE OVER 100 DIFFERENT TYPES OR BREEDS OF PET RABBIT.

RABBIT

Rabbits make great pets because they are cuddly, playful and easy to take care of. They are also gentle animals that enjoy being stroked. Always stroke them in the direction that the fur grows.

HOME SWEET HOME

Most pet rabbits live outdoors in hutches, but they enjoy hopping about on the grass inside a run made from wood and wire mesh. Rabbits are clever animals so they can also learn to use a litter tray and live indoors like a cat.

BIG & SMALL

When you buy a rabbit, ask how big it will grow. Small rabbits weigh about as much as a bag of sugar. But some rabbits will grow too big for you to pick up. A big rabbit can eat ten times more food than a small one.

RABBITS' EARS STAND UP TO LISTEN FOR DANGER.

THUMPER

Rabbits thump their back legs on the ground to warn other rabbits of danger.

RABBITS CAN LIVE FOR 6–12 YEARS AND CAN HAVE 6 OR 7 BABIES AT A TIME.

19

GOLDFISH

Goldfish make excellent pets because they do not cost very much and they do not make a noise or a mess. They are hardy fish that do not need a lot of attention and can live for a long time.

INDOOR PONDS

Goldfish are best kept in open pools outside, but can adapt to living in tanks indoors. They need plenty of plants to put oxygen into the water and they like to live with other goldfish or coldwater fishes. Goldfish feed on plants and small animals.

COLOURFUL GOLDFISH

There are over 125 kinds of goldfish, in all sorts of colours, from the typical orange ones to the black moor or the blue Shubunkins.

FISH CAN HEAR WELL AND PICK UP VIBRATIONS IN THE WATER.

SMALL BOWLS DO NOT HOLD ENOUGH OXYGEN FOR GOLDFISH.

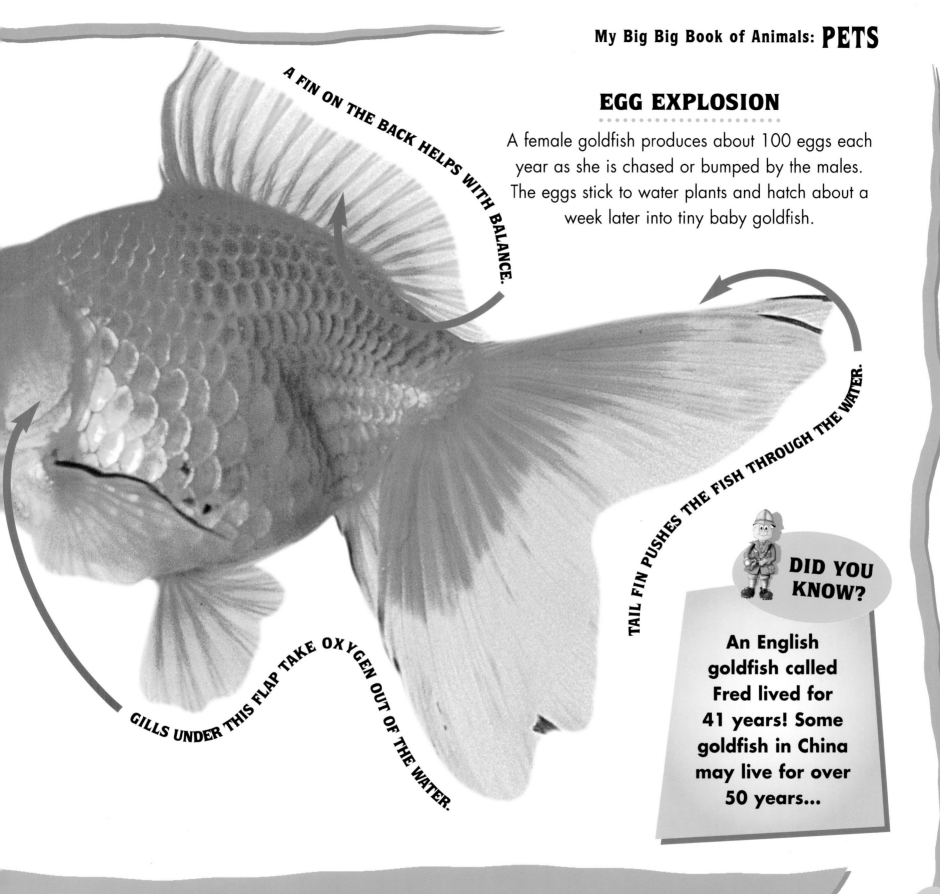

A FIN ON THE BACK HELPS WITH BALANCE.

EGG EXPLOSION

A female goldfish produces about 100 eggs each year as she is chased or bumped by the males. The eggs stick to water plants and hatch about a week later into tiny baby goldfish.

TAIL FIN PUSHES THE FISH THROUGH THE WATER.

GILLS UNDER THIS FLAP TAKE OXYGEN OUT OF THE WATER.

DID YOU KNOW?

An English goldfish called Fred lived for 41 years! Some goldfish in China may live for over 50 years...

One breed of cat, called the sphynx, has no hair at all. It catches cold very easily and usually stays indoors to keep warm.

A CAT'S PUPILS CLOSE TO A SLIT IN BRIGHT LIGHT OR WHEN THE CAT IS ANGRY.

WHISKERS FOR FEELING THEIR WAY IN THE DARK.

CLAWS ARE HIDDEN INSIDE POCKETS OF SKIN IN ITS FEET.

GOT TO SCRATCH

Pet cats often scratch the furniture unless you give them a piece of wood or a scratching post to use instead. Scratching helps a cat to sharpen its claws. Cats can pull in their claws, which stops them wearing down.

THE LONG TAIL HELPS A CAT TO BALANCE.

CATS SLEEP FOR ABOUT 15 HOURS A DAY.

CAT

Cats are clean, calm and loving pets. They don't need to be taken for walks but they do like to go out by themselves. Kittens and younger cats are very playful but older cats spend a lot of time asleep!

KITTY CAT

Young cats are called kittens. They cannot see or hear when they are first born but they can look after themselves when they are about eight weeks old.

PLAYFUL POUNCE

Pet cats and kittens pounce on things just like a wild cat pounces on its prey. Before they pounce, they crouch down and slowly creep closer, without making a sound.

A CAT CAN LIVE FOR 15 YEARS – ONE RECORD-BREAKING CAT LIVED FOR 28 YEARS!

MONKEY

Playful, clever, noisy monkeys leap through the rainforests, clinging tightly to the branches with their long fingers and tails. There is plenty of fruit, leaves and insects for them to eat and they can escape from enemies by living high in the trees.

WASH AND BRUSH-UP

Monkeys carefully groom each other's fur, picking out any dirt or lice and cleaning cuts and scratches. Grooming helps the monkeys to relax and stay good friends with the other monkeys in their group.

STINK FIGHTS

Lemurs are related to monkeys but they have a smaller brain and a far better sense of smell. Ring-tailed lemurs rub scent on their tails and have stink fights by waving their smelly tails at each other.

LEMURS LIVE ONLY IN MADAGASCAR, AN ISLAND OFF THE COAST OF AFRICA.

A MONKEY'S EYES FACE FORWARDS TO HELP IT SEE A SAFE PATH THROUGH TREES.

OPEN WIDE

Some monkeys, such as macaques, have cheek pouches, which extend down the sides of the neck. This helps them to collect a lot of food quickly. Then they find a safe place to eat the food.

HEAVY BROW AND NOSE RIDGES HELP TO PROTECT THE EYES AND NOSE.

CHEEK POUCHES STORE FOOD.

STRONG, GRIPPING FINGERS HOLD BRANCHES AND FOOD.

THICK FUR KEEPS OUT THE COLD AND WET.

DID YOU KNOW?

Some monkeys, such as spider monkeys and howler monkeys, have special gripping tails, called prehensile tails. They grip the branches tightly like an extra hand.

SPIDER MONKEYS SOMETIMES WALK ON TWO LEGS LIKE YOU DO.

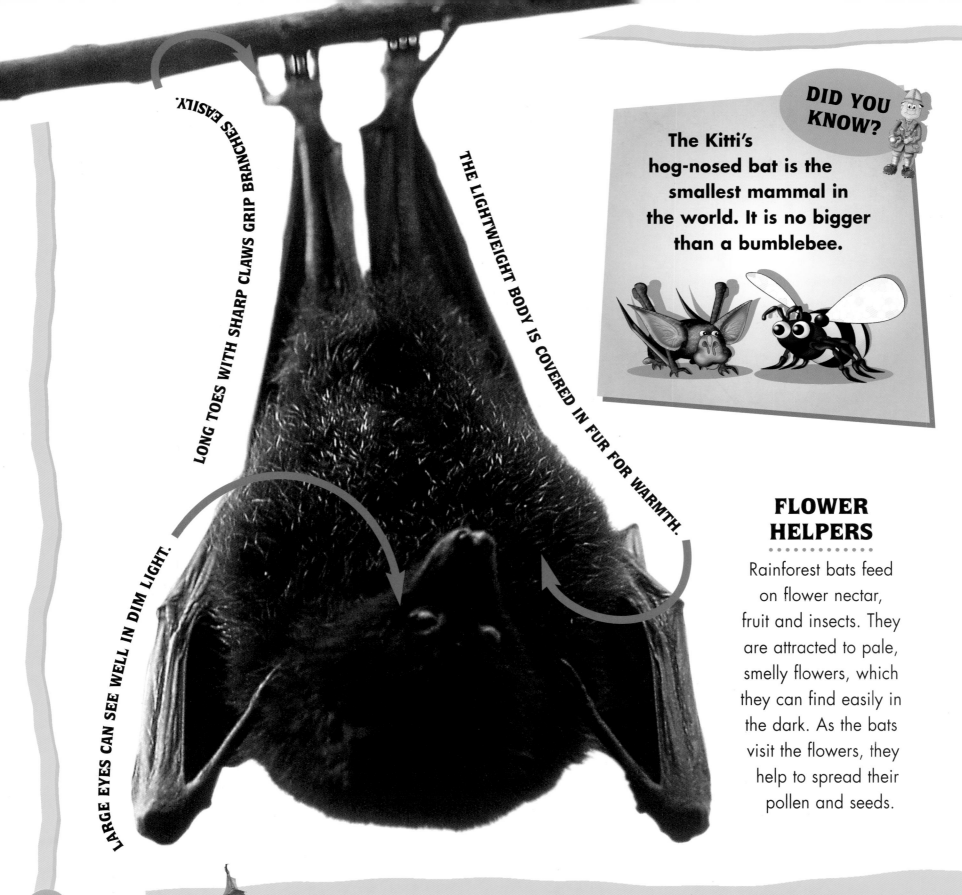

LONG TOES WITH SHARP CLAWS GRIP BRANCHES EASILY.

THE LIGHTWEIGHT BODY IS COVERED IN FUR FOR WARMTH.

LARGE EYES CAN SEE WELL IN DIM LIGHT.

The Kitti's hog-nosed bat is the smallest mammal in the world. It is no bigger than a bumblebee.

FLOWER HELPERS

Rainforest bats feed on flower nectar, fruit and insects. They are attracted to pale, smelly flowers, which they can find easily in the dark. As the bats visit the flowers, they help to spread their pollen and seeds.

NEARLY ONE QUARTER OF ALL MAMMALS ARE BATS!

BAT

Bats are the only mammals that can fly. Bats are found in most places, maybe even your attic, but you will also find them flying through the trees in the rainforests of the world.

MAKE ROOM FOR ME!

Bats sleep hanging upside down in a resting place, called a roost. There they also wash and groom themselves by hanging from one foot and combing their fur with the other foot. Bats are very clean animals.

STRETCHY WINGS

A bat's wings are made of thin skin stretched over a framework of long arm and finger bones. When a bat rests, it often folds its wings around its body, like a tent.

THERE ARE ABOUT 1,000 DIFFERENT KINDS OF BAT.

TREE FROG

Tree frogs have small, lightweight bodies and sticky toes to help them climb through the rainforest. Their large eyes face forwards to help them judge distances when climbing or catching prey. Some tree frogs can fly and can glide up to 15 metres between rainforest trees.

DON'T EAT ME!

The bright colours of poison arrow tree frogs warn enemies to leave them alone. Rainforest people sometimes use the poison on their arrows to help them kill monkeys and birds.

FOOT GLUE

Tree frogs can cling upside down in the forest for hours at a time using special rounded pads on their fingers and toes that are filled with a sticky 'glue'. This helps them to grip wet leaves and other slippery and slimy surfaces.

GLASS FROGS HAVE SEE-THROUGH SKIN SO YOU CAN SEE SOME OF THEIR BONES.

TADPOLE CARRIER

Poison arrow frogs carry their tadpoles on their backs to a stream
or a pool of water among the leaves of a rainforest plant.
The tadpoles stick to the adult's back so they do not fall off.

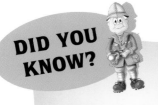
BRIGHT COLOURS ACT AS A WARNING AGAINST THE POISON IN THE FROG'S SKIN.

LARGE EYES BULGE OUT OF THE TOP OF THE FROG'S HEAD.

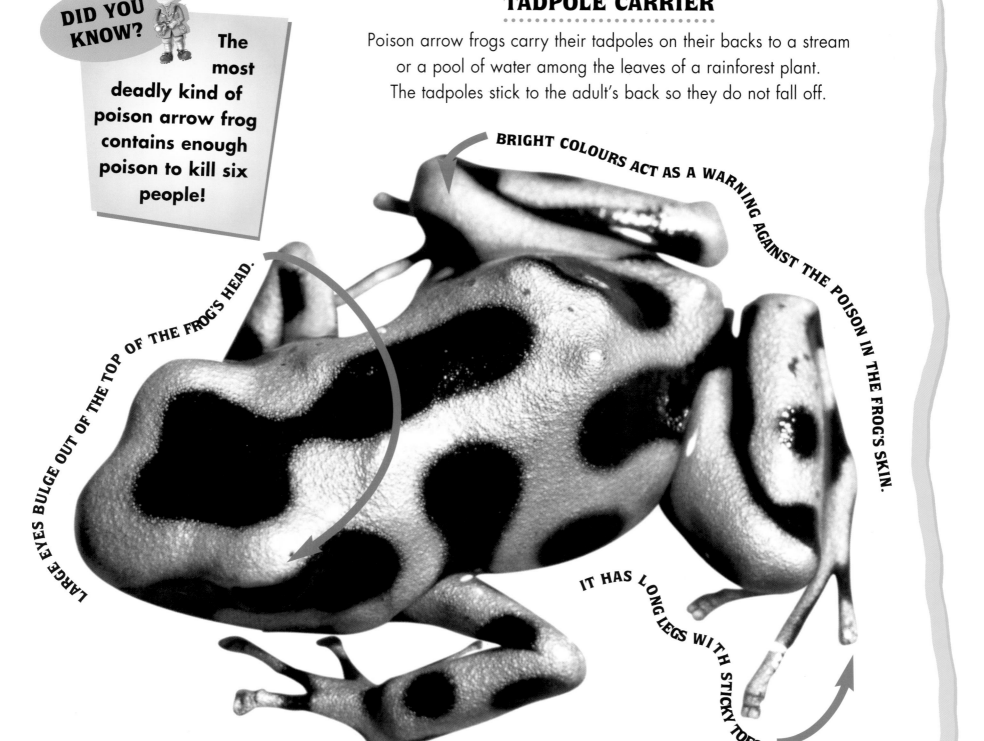

IT HAS LONG LEGS WITH STICKY TOES.

Elephants love to plaster themselves in mud, which cools their skin, helps to heal cuts and protects them from insect bites. It also helps to stop their skin from getting dry and cracked.

SMALL EYES ARE PROTECTED BY LONG EYELASHES.

IT HAS WRINKLY SKIN, WITH HARDLY ANY HAIR.

FEET WITH DEEP RIDGES HELP THE ELEPHANT GRIP THE GROUND.

THE LONG, BENDY TRUNK HAS ONE FINGER AT THE TIP.

AN ELEPHANT CAN LIVE AS LONG AS A PERSON, ABOUT 70 YEARS OR SO.

ELEPHANT

Rainforest elephants move around quietly and can quickly disappear among the trees. They are vegetarians and spend about 16 hours a day choosing, picking and eating their plant food.

LIVING TOGETHER

Asian elephants live in small family groups of between four and eight elephants. A wise old female elephant usually leads the group. She decides when they will eat, drink and rest and protects them from danger.

TRICKY TRUNK

An elephant's trunk is its nose and top lip joined together into a long, bendy tube. It uses its trunk to breathe, pick things up, squirt water, feel and smell things, and make trumpeting sounds. A baby elephant takes a long time to learn how to use its trunk properly.

FEMALE ELEPHANTS CARRY THEIR BABIES INSIDE THEM FOR NEARLY TWO YEARS.

PARROT

Flying about in noisy, screeching flocks, parrots are among the most colourful animals in the rainforest. Many of them are rare today because the rainforests where they live have been cut down. Macaws are the largest parrots in the world.

BIGGEST PARROT

PARROTS ARE INTELLIGENT BIRDS THAT CAN BE TRAINED TO SPEAK.

The scarlet macaw is the biggest parrot in South America. Its strong hooked beak has sharp cutting edges that work like nutcrackers to split open tough nuts and seeds. Such a powerful bill can even crack open very hard Brazil nuts.

FINGER FOOD

Parrots are the only birds that use their feet to hold their food up to their bills. They use their strong tongues to prise out the flesh of fruits and nuts from their shells.

CHAMPION CLIMBER

Parrots have two toes pointing forwards and two pointing backwards. This gives them a very strong grip on branches and helps them to use their feet to hold things. When they climb through the treetops, parrots also use their bill like a grappling hook to hold onto branches.

BABY PARROTS ARE BLIND, NAKED AND HELPLESS WHEN THEY HATCH OUT OF THEIR EGGS.

PARROTS CAN OPEN THEIR BILL VERY WIDE TO PICK AND EAT LARGE FRUIT AND NUTS.

DID YOU KNOW?

The hanging parrot hangs upside down from branches to sleep, like a bat! This may help it to hide from enemies that hunt at night.

MACAWS HAVE BRIGHT AND COLOURFUL FEATHERS.

THIS HYACINTH MACAW IS RARE.

A MACAW COULD BITE OFF A HUMAN FINGER WITH ITS POWERFUL BILL.

DID YOU KNOW?

A tiger may be longer than a car and weigh more than two people!

HUNTING MACHINE

Tigers usually hunt at night for animals such as deer and wild pigs. They have huge, pointed front teeth to seize their prey and deliver a killing bite to the neck. A tiger's sharp cheek teeth help to slice up its food.

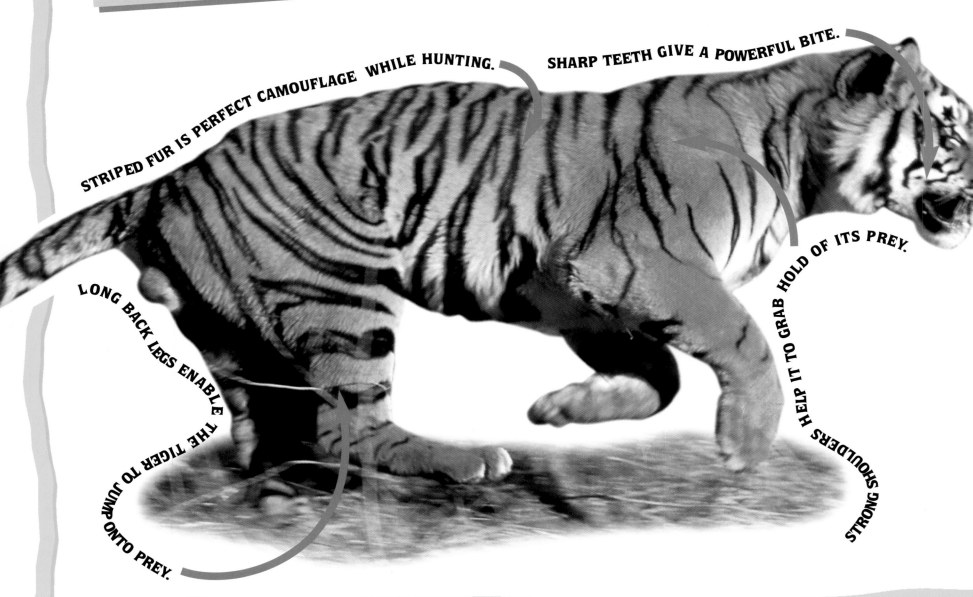

STRIPED FUR IS PERFECT CAMOUFLAGE WHILE HUNTING.

SHARP TEETH GIVE A POWERFUL BITE.

STRONG SHOULDERS HELP IT TO GRAB HOLD OF ITS PREY.

LONG BACK LEGS ENABLE THE TIGER TO JUMP ONTO PREY.

TIGERS CAN SEE ABOUT SIX TIMES BETTER THAN PEOPLE IN DIM LIGHT.

TIGER

Tigers are the biggest and strongest cats in the world. They are also the only big cats that are striped all over. Tigers are rare because the rainforests in which they live are being cut down and because they are hunted for their fur.

MAGIC STRIPES

The beautiful black stripes on a tiger's coat help to camouflage it among trees, bushes and grasses. This means a tiger can creep really close to its prey without being seen.

RARE WHITE TIGERS ARE BORN WITHOUT ANY ORANGE IN THEIR FUR.

FACE PAINT

Every tiger has a different pattern of stripes on its face. This helps scientists and conservationists to tell one tiger from another.

TIGERS CAN ROAR BUT THEY CANNOT PURR. THEIR ROAR CAN BE HEARD UP TO 3.2 KM AWAY.

35

GORILLA

Gorillas live in peaceful family groups in the rainforests of Africa. A strong male gorilla leads the group. Male gorillas are about twice the size of females and may weigh almost as much as three men!

PLAYFUL BABIES

Young gorillas spend most of their time exploring and playing. They wrestle, chase each other and climb trees and scramble over the adults. This helps them to test their strength, build up their muscles and learn how to get on with other gorillas.

BIG BRAIN

When you look into the eyes of a gorilla, you can see an intelligent animal staring back at you. Big male gorillas stare hard at enemies or troublemakers in their group to show that they are in charge.

A GORILLA HAS A BIG HEAD BECAUSE IT HAS A LARGE BRAIN, A STRONG SKULL AND BIG JAW MUSCLES.

A NEWBORN GORILLA WEIGHS ONLY HALF AS MUCH AS A HUMAN BABY.

DID YOU KNOW?

A gorilla's fingers are thicker than yours - about the size of bananas!

BONY RIDGES HELP TO PROTECT THE EYES.

THICK FUR KEEPS A GORILLA WARM AT NIGHT.

A GORILLA'S ARMS ARE LONGER THAN ITS LEGS.

A GORILLA USUALLY WALKS ON ALL FOURS.

LAZY DAYS

Gorillas spend their days slowly walking through the rainforest, stopping every so often for tasty snacks of plants, such as wild celery, wild ginger or nettles. After lunch they have a nap for two or three hours to let their food go down.

GORILLAS LOOK SCARY BUT ARE REALLY GENTLE ANIMALS.

SCHOOL FRIENDS

Many dolphins live in small groups called schools or pods. The pod members help to look after each other if a predator attacks or if one of the dolphins is sick or injured.

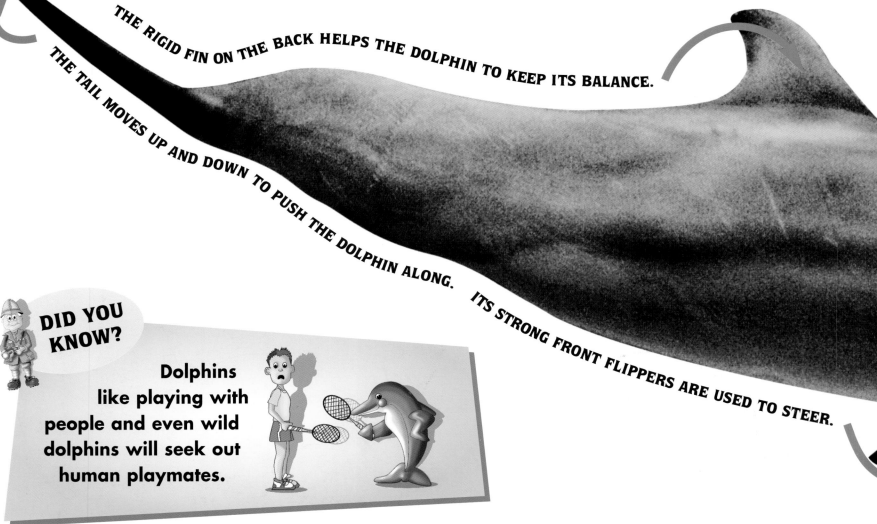

THE RIGID FIN ON THE BACK HELPS THE DOLPHIN TO KEEP ITS BALANCE.

THE TAIL MOVES UP AND DOWN TO PUSH THE DOLPHIN ALONG.

ITS STRONG FRONT FLIPPERS ARE USED TO STEER.

DID YOU KNOW?

Dolphins like playing with people and even wild dolphins will seek out human playmates.

DOLPHINS ARE REALLY A KIND OF SMALL WHALE WITH TEETH.

DOLPHIN

Dolphins are fast-swimming, intelligent mammals that live in coastal waters and oceans. They have to come to the surface to breathe air through the blowhole on the top of their heads, but they sleep, mate and even give birth underwater.

SOUND SIGNALS

Dolphins can pinpoint prey and steer clear of obstacles by using echoes. They make rapid clicks, which bounce off things around them and go back to their ears. The dolphin's brain converts these sound echoes into a detailed sound picture of its surroundings. This is called echolocation.

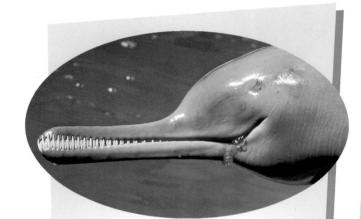

RIVER DOLPHINS

Most dolphins live in seas and oceans, but some live in rivers, such as the Amazon in South America, and the Ganges in India. River dolphins have longer snouts and are almost blind, relying on sound echoes to find food.

A STREAMLINED SHAPE HELPS THE DOLPHIN TO SWIM FAST.

A DOLPHIN HAS UP TO 252 SHARP TEETH.

SEAL & SEA LION

Seals and sea lions are sleek, fast-moving hunters that twist and turn like graceful acrobats under the water. They eat mainly fish and squid. Seals and sea lions have to come onto land to rest, mate and give birth.

SEALS AND SEA LIONS HAVE LARGE EYES THAT SEE CLEARLY IN WATER AS WELL AS OUT.

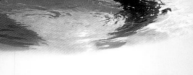

FLIPPER WALK

Sea lions and fur seals move more easily on land than true seals because they can bring their back flippers forward and walk on all fours. They also have longer legs than true seals.

EAR, EAR

True seals like this pup have no ear flaps on the sides of the head. Sea lions and fur seals have small outer ears. True seals are terrific swimmers and deep divers. They swim with their back flippers, whereas sea lions and fur seals swim with their front flippers.

SEALS AND SEA LIONS ARE MAMMALS, JUST LIKE YOU, BUT WITH A HAIRY SKIN AND FLIPPERS!

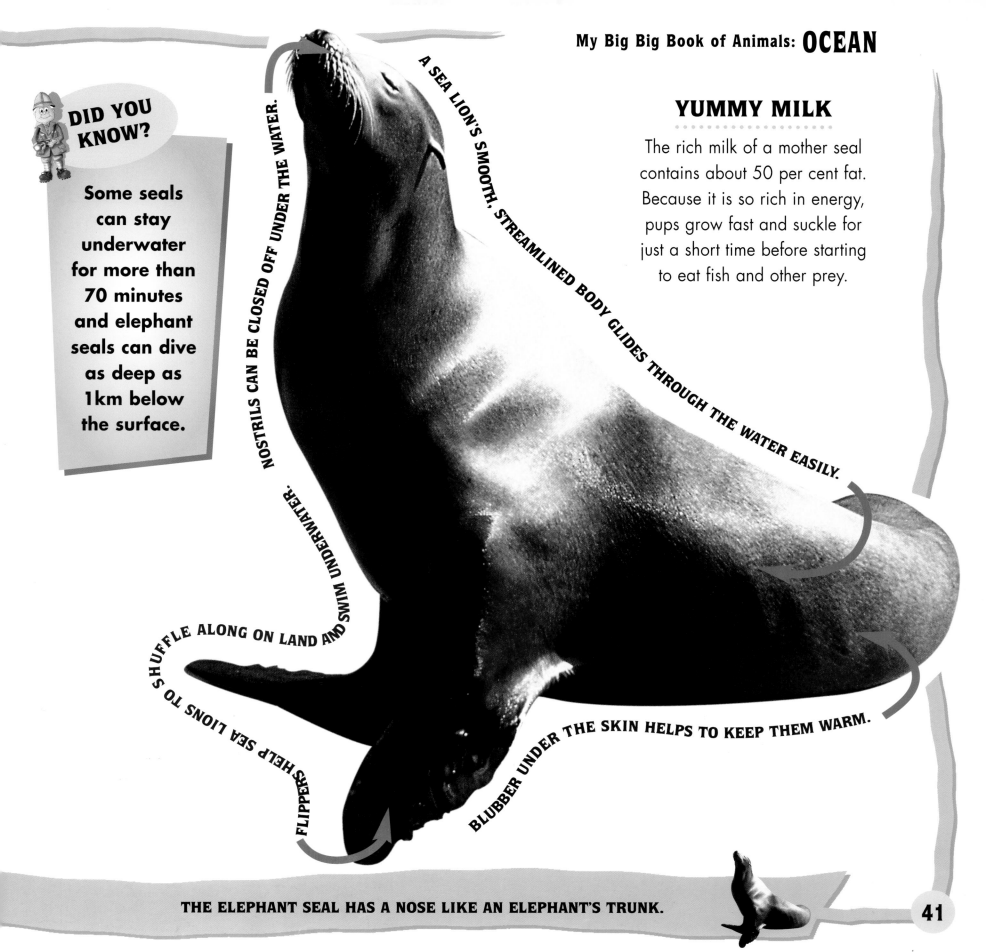

DID YOU KNOW?

Some seals can stay underwater for more than 70 minutes and elephant seals can dive as deep as 1km below the surface.

YUMMY MILK

The rich milk of a mother seal contains about 50 per cent fat. Because it is so rich in energy, pups grow fast and suckle for just a short time before starting to eat fish and other prey.

A SEA LION'S SMOOTH, STREAMLINED BODY GLIDES THROUGH THE WATER EASILY.

NOSTRILS CAN BE CLOSED OFF UNDER THE WATER.

FLIPPERS HELP SEA LIONS TO SHUFFLE ALONG ON LAND AND SWIM UNDERWATER.

BLUBBER UNDER THE SKIN HELPS TO KEEP THEM WARM.

THE ELEPHANT SEAL HAS A NOSE LIKE AN ELEPHANT'S TRUNK.

FRIENDLY SHARKS

Most sharks are harmless to people. More people die from bee stings or lightning strikes than from shark attacks. Great white sharks do sometimes attack people though, perhaps because they look like seals swimming near the surface.

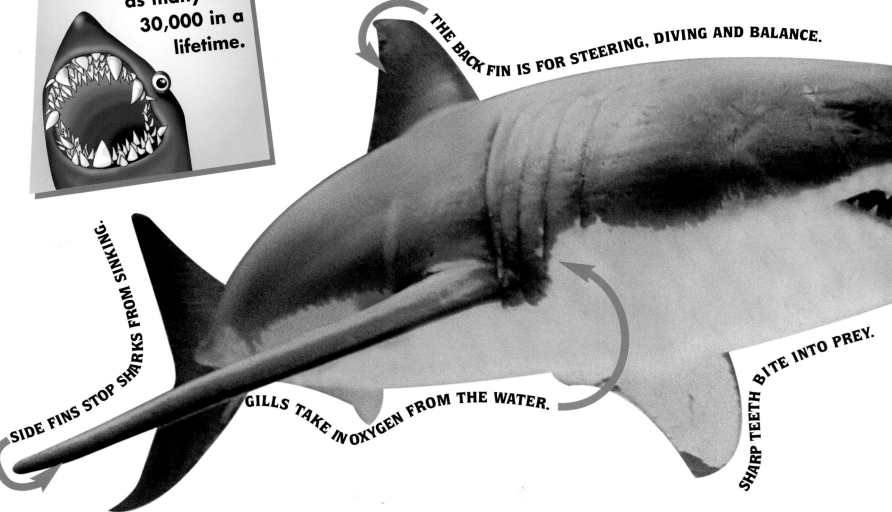

THE BACK FIN IS FOR STEERING, DIVING AND BALANCE.

SIDE FINS STOP SHARKS FROM SINKING.

GILLS TAKE IN OXYGEN FROM THE WATER.

SHARP TEETH BITE INTO PREY.

MOST OPEN OCEAN SHARKS HAVE TO KEEP SWIMMING OR THEY WILL DROWN.

SHARK

Sharks are powerful predators that swim through the world's oceans. Their skeletons are made of tough, rubbery cartilage, not bone like yours. They have gill slits behind the head instead of a gill cover.

POINTED NOSE AND STREAMLINED BODY FOR FAST SWIMMING.

BABY PURSE

Small sharks called dogfish lay eggs in tough egg cases called mermaid's purses. You may find these washed up on the beach. The long tendrils curl around seaweeds to stop the egg case being washed away.

WHITE MONSTER

The great white shark is a huge and powerful hunter with razor-sharp teeth. Its teeth have saw edges, like steak knives. The colour of a great white shark makes it hard to see in the water so it can take its victims by surprise.

THE GIGANTIC WHALE SHARK IS THE WORLD'S LARGEST FISH. LUCKILY IT IS HARMLESS!

FISH

From freezing polar oceans to warm tropical seas, fish live in all the world's oceans. They swim using their tails and body fins and breathe through their gills, which take oxygen out of the water.

THE GILLS ARE UNDER THIS BONY GILL COVER, CALLED AN OPERCULUM.

SMELLY MESSAGES

Salmon grow into adults in the ocean, but when the time comes to breed, they swim back to the rivers where they were born. They recognise the place by the smell of the water. This special journey is called migration.

BREATHING UNDERWATER

Fish draw water into the mouth and pump it over the gills at the back of the head. Oxygen passes into the fish's blood and the water flows out through the gill slits.

STRONG TAIL FIN PUSHES THE FISH THROUGH THE WATER.

A SLIMY COATING HELPS THE FISH TO GLIDE THROUGH THE WATER.

SOME FISH PROTECT THEIR YOUNG BY HOLDING THEM IN THEIR MOUTHS.

CORAL KALEIDOSCOPE

Coral reefs have plenty of food and hiding places so they are full of colourful fish such as this yellow tang. The tang is a sort of surgeon fish, with a sharp, knife-like scalpel at the base of the tail, for defence.

A STREAMLINED SHAPE HELPS THIS FISH SHOOT THROUGH THE WATER AT ABOUT 21 KM/H.

THE SCALES OVERLAP, LIKE THE TILES ON A ROOF.

DID YOU KNOW?

Flying fish can glide above the waves for up to 50 metres by beating their large front fins like wings.

ADULT EELS LIVE IN RIVERS BUT GO BACK TO THE SEA TO BREED.

CLEVER CHANGES

A flatfish starts life shaped like a normal fish. But as it grows, one eye moves to the other side of the head, the mouth usually twists round and the body flattens. As it changes, the little fish sinks to the sea bed.

PATTERN OF SPOTS AND BLOTCHES BREAK UP THE OUTLINE OF THE BODY TO GIVE GOOD CAMOUFLAGE.

TAIL FIN TO PUSH THE FISH ALONG.

FINS ARE ROUND THE EDGES OF THE BODY.

THE UNDERSIDE OF FLATFISH IS A PALE COLOUR AND NOT CAMOUFLAGED.

FLATFISH

Flatfish really are as flat as pancakes! They live on the sea bed, often burying themselves in the sand or mud. All flatfish are meat-eaters. Some hunt fish, while others catch worms and shellfish.

CAMOUFLAGE COLOURS

This plaice can change the pattern of colours on its skin so it matches the background perfectly. When it lies flat on the sea bed and keeps still, it becomes almost invisible.

NOSTRILS ARE ON THE SAME SIDE OF THE BODY AS THE EYES.

GOGGLE EYES

A flatfish has both its eyes on the same side of its head. Its mouth is also twisted round so a flatfish looks as if it is grinning at you! It lies down on its blind side.

THE EGGS OF FLATFISH CONTAIN DROPLETS OF OIL TO HELP THEM FLOAT NEAR THE SURFACE.

SEAHORSE

A seahorse is a strange fish with a head like a horse and a curly tail like a monkey for gripping things tightly. It also has two skeletons – one inside its body and one outside.

BABY MINDER

A female seahorse lays her eggs in a pouch on the front of the male's body. He looks after the eggs for a few weeks until they hatch into baby seahorses.

THE SEAHORSE CURLS ITS TAIL AROUND PLANTS FOR SUPPORT.

WEEDY DRAGON

The leafy sea dragon grows pretend seaweed all over its body to help it hide from its enemies. It cannot swim very fast but its brilliant camouflage disguises its real shape and protects it from danger.

THE SEAHORSE CURLS ITS TAIL TO SINK AND STRAIGHTENS ITS TAIL TO RISE UP.

HORSEY HOOVER

A seahorse sucks up shrimps with its long hollow jaws. This makes a clicking noise which can be heard some distance away. Seahorses have to swallow their food whole because they have no teeth.

DID YOU KNOW?

A young seahorse eats up to 3,500 shrimps in a day, but it has no teeth and no stomach!

SMALL FINS ON THE HEAD FOR STEERING.

BULGING EYES LOOK IN DIFFERENT DIRECTIONS TO SPOT PREY AND DANGER.

ITS BACK FIN BEATS AT 20-30 TIMES A SECOND.

IT HAS BODY ARMOUR OF BONY PLATES FOR EXTRA PROTECTION.

SEAHORSES CAN CHANGE COLOUR TO BLEND IN WITH THE BACKGROUND.

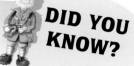
The boxer crab wears a sea anemone on each pincer. It uses the stinging cells of the anemones to scare off enemies.

BEST LEG FORWARD

Crabs move sideways and some of them can scuttle along quite fast. Swimming crabs use their back pair of legs like oars to row themselves through the water. The legs are flat and fringed with hairs to push more water aside on each stroke.

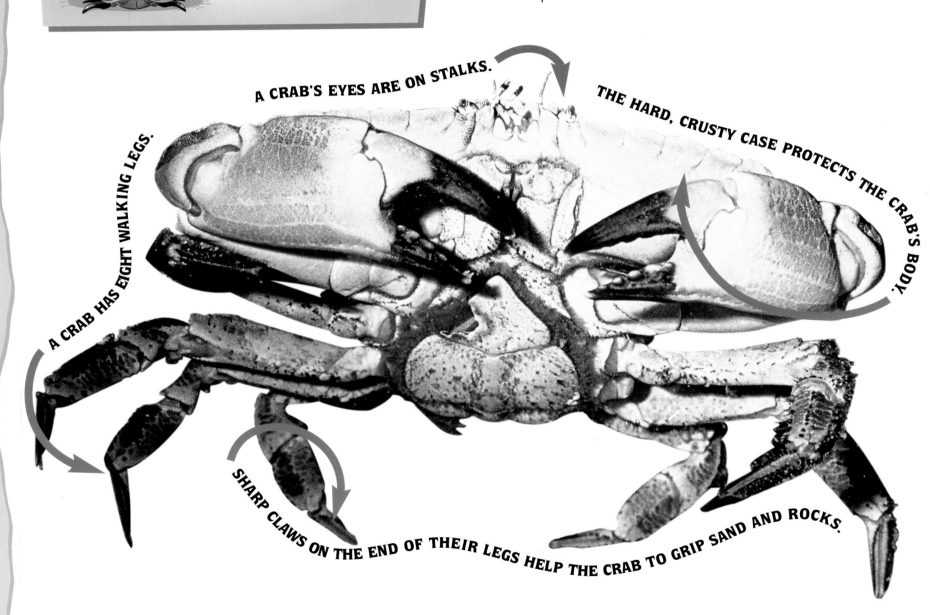

A CRAB'S EYES ARE ON STALKS.

THE HARD, CRUSTY CASE PROTECTS THE CRAB'S BODY.

A CRAB HAS EIGHT WALKING LEGS.

SHARP CLAWS ON THE END OF THEIR LEGS HELP THE CRAB TO GRIP SAND AND ROCKS.

CRABS CAN GROW NEW LEGS IF ONE BREAKS OFF.

CRAB

A crab's body is covered in a hard, protective case and it has ten legs. The front pair of legs are big pincers. As crabs grow, they wriggle out of their old, tight body cases to make way for new, bigger ones.

MOBILE HOME

The back part of a hermit crab's body does not have a hard case, like other crabs. So it lives inside empty seashells to protect its soft body parts. As the hermit crab grows bigger, it has to find a bigger shell to live in.

PINCER POWER

Crabs use their big pincers to attack enemies and to eat their food. A crab's pincers contain the white meat while its body shell contains the dark meat.

CRABS ARE SCAVENGERS THAT FEED ON DEAD BODIES AND DEBRIS.

OWL

Most owls are night-time hunters that catch animals such as mice and small birds. There are over 200 different kinds of owl in the world. Most live in woodlands and have brown speckled feathers for camouflage. Others live in deserts, grasslands or snowy places.

SNOWY OWLS CAN KILL AS MANY AS TEN LEMMINGS A DAY.

SNOW FEATHERS

The white feathers of the snowy owl match the snowy places in which it lives. The feathers also help to keep the owl warm and protect its legs from the bites and scratches of its live prey.

TWISTY NECK

Owls have twice as many bones in their neck as you do. This is why they can turn their head nearly three quarters of the way around to look behind them. A twisty neck helps an owl to spot its prey.

OWLS HOOT TO ATTRACT A MATE AND WARN OTHER OWLS TO STAY OUT OF THEIR AREA.

OWLS HAVE VERY KEEN EYESIGHT AND HEARING.

THE HOOKED BEAK HELPS THE OWL TO EAT.

CAMOUFLAGE COLOURS PROTECT IT WHEN IT RESTS.

NEEDLE-SHARP CURVED TALONS TO GRIP PREY.

COUGH, COUGH

Owls cough up the bits of their food they cannot digest, such as fur and bones. These bits of food stick together to make owl pellets. You may find a lot of pellets under the trees where owls sleep during the day.

DID YOU KNOW?

Owls have special fringes on their wing feathers. This muffles the sound of their wings so they can fly almost silently.

A TAWNY OWL CAN SEE TWO OR THREE TIMES BETTER IN THE DARK THAN A PERSON.

DID YOU KNOW?

The Harpy Eagle can fly up to 80 km/h as it chases monkeys through the rainforests.

CARING PARENTS

Eagles build stick nests called eyries, adding to the same nest year after year. To feed their young, they tear up their prey into bite-sized pieces, which are easy for them to swallow.

ITS STRONG WINGS ENABLE IT TO FLY HIGH IN THE SKY WHILE LOOKING FOR A MEAL.

A HOOKED BILL CAN TEAR APART THE FLESH OF ITS PREY.

CURVED TALONS ARE AS SHARP AS RAZORS.

BALD EAGLES ARE THE NATIONAL BIRD OF THE USA.

EAGLE

Eagles are the most powerful birds of prey and they are fantastic flyers. Their long, broad wings help them to stay up in the air for hours. They hunt during the day, catching their prey in their sharp, curved talons.

AN EAGLE CAN SPOT A RABBIT FROM A DISTANCE OF ABOUT 1.5 KM AWAY.

UP AND AWAY

Eagles have enormous wings, with big muscles to help them soar high into the air. The feathers at the tips of the wings spread out like fingers to help the eagle push and steer through the air.

CIRCUS EAGLE

This eagle's name - Bateleur - means 'tightrope walker' because it tilts from side to side as it flies, just like a real tightrope walker trying to balance on a thin wire in a circus.

THE BALD EAGLE BUILDS THE BIGGEST NEST IN THE WORLD.

OSTRICH

An ostrich is the biggest and tallest bird in the world. It is also the fastest animal on two legs. An ostrich cannot fly so it has to run fast to escape from enemies. It lives on the grasslands of Africa, moving around in groups in search for food.

TWO PLUS TWO

An ostrich has long legs with powerful muscles and only two toes on each foot.

SPOT THE DIFFERENCE

The male ostrich is bigger than the female. He has black feathers and a pink neck and legs. The female is a greyish-brown colour for camouflage. The male's feathers were once highly prized. They were used on ladies' hats and other fashion items.

AN OSTRICH FEATHER WAS THE SYMBOL OF JUSTICE IN ANCIENT EGYPT.

HUGE EYES SPOT DANGER FROM FAR AWAY.

BEAK OPENS VERY WIDE TO PECK UP FOOD.

AN OSTRICH'S HEIGHT HELPS IT TO SEE DANGER COMING.

LONG, BENDY NECK REACHES FOOD ON THE GROUND.

DID YOU KNOW?

An ostrich can sprint along at up to 72 km/h - that's twice as fast as a human sprinter running a race.

BIG AND STRONG

Female ostriches lay the biggest eggs of any bird. One ostrich egg is the same size as 24 chickens' eggs! The eggshell is so strong that a person can stand on an ostrich's egg without breaking it.

SOME PEOPLE BELIEVE THE SHELLS OF OSTRICH EGGS HAVE MAGICAL POWERS.

IT HAS THREE LAYERS OF OILY, OVERLAPPING, WATERPROOF FEATHERS.

A SPIKY TONGUE TO CATCH SLIPPERY FISH.

A THICK LAYER OF FAT UNDER THE SKIN TO KEEP WARM.

HATS ON HEADS

Some penguins have colourful ear tufts, head crests or patches of colour on their faces. These help them to recognise other penguins of the same kind and to attract a mate.

THE LITTLE BLUE, OR FAIRY, PENGUIN WEIGHS LITTLE MORE THAN A BAG OF SUGAR.

PENGUIN

Penguins spend most of their lives swimming through the oceans in the southern part of the globe. Every year they come out of the water to moult their feathers and lay their eggs.

SAFETY IN NUMBERS

Many penguins nest on the ice that forms around the coast of Antarctica in winter, as well as on nearby islands. Here they are safe from most predators. Millions of birds may nest together.

FLIPPER POWER

Penguins cannot fly, but they use their stiff, narrow wings to 'fly' underwater. Big webbed feet also help the penguin to steer while swimming.

MALE EMPEROR PENGUINS BALANCE THEIR EGGS ON THEIR FEET TO KEEP THEM WARM.

PEACOCK

Wild peacocks live in the hilly forests and farmlands of India, Pakistan and Sri Lanka but they also live in parks and gardens all over the world. Male peacocks are famous for their fantastic feathers, whereas female peacocks, peahens, are dull in comparison.

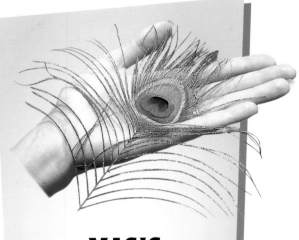

MAGIC FEATHERS

The colours of a peacock's 'eye' feathers change as the feathers move. This is because of the special shape of the feathers and the way they reflect the light.

WHAT A TAIL!

A colourful male peacock tries to impress a female by fanning out his tail into a shimmering curtain of green and blue eyes. Female peacocks mate with the males that have the most stunning fans.

MAY THE BEST BIRD WIN

In the breeding season, a male peacock claims a special area called his territory, where he shows off to the females. He has fierce fights with any males that try to invade his territory. Some fights last for a whole day or more!

PEAHENS CAN BE HYPNOTISED BY THE MASS OF STARING EYES ON THE MALE'S TAIL.

THE FEATHERS ON A PEACOCK'S HEAD LOOK LIKE A ROYAL CROWN.

DID YOU KNOW? At the end of the mating season, the male's beautiful tail falls out!

ROUNDED WINGS ARE NOT OFTEN USED FOR FLYING.

MALES FOLD UP THEIR TAILS SO THEY TRAIL BEHIND THEM.

PEAHENS ARE CAMOUFLAGED SO ENEMIES WILL NOT SPOT THEM.

EYES ON THE SIDES OF ITS HEAD WATCH OUT FOR DANGER.

LONG NARROW WINGS HELP IT TO GLIDE THROUGH THE AIR.

IT HAS WEBBED FEET FOR SWIMMING.

THIS YOUNG SEAGULL HAS SPECKLED BROWN FEATHERS.

FEATHERED DUSTBIN

Herring gulls will eat almost anything, from fish and crabs to worms and baby birds. They also peck through the rubbish we throw away on rubbish tips to find tasty morsels to eat.

HERRING GULLS DROP MUSSELS FROM A HEIGHT TO BREAK THEM OPEN.

SEAGULL

Seagulls are good at gliding and soaring high above the sea or the cliffs along the shore. Many of them also live inland, especially in winter when they feed from rubbish tips.

CHOCOLATE HEAD

In winter, the black-headed gull has a white head with a black spot behind its eyes. But in the breeding season, it grows a hood of chocolate-brown feathers. This makes its head show up during its courtship display.

THE SAME BUT DIFFERENT

While they are growing up, gulls are a different colour from their parents. Most young gulls have mottled brown feathers, which helps them to hide from foxes, bigger gulls and other enemies.

SEAGULLS HAVE ONE PARTNER AND USUALLY PAIR FOR LIFE.

PIGEON

There are around 300 different kinds of pigeon. Most of them live in trees and feed on seeds and fruits but some live in towns and cities. They come in variety of colours from dark grey to white all over.

PIGEON POWER

City pigeons are tame enough to perch on people and can be fed by hand. There is plenty of food for them in cities. They nest on buildings, which are like the cliffs they nest on in the wild.

DRY CLEANING

Pigeons have special feathers that break up to form a powder. They use this to keep their feathers clean and tidy.

RACING PIGEONS CAN FLY AT AROUND 70 KM/H.

PIGEONS COO, WHICH IS THEIR WAY OF TALKING TO EACH OTHER.

A STRONG, CHUNKY BILL FOR EATING SEEDS AND FRUITS.

THEY CAN DRINK WATER WITHOUT RAISING THEIR HEADS.

A PLUMP BODY WITH SMALL HEAD AND SHORT LEGS.

SOFT, DENSE FEATHERS.

DID YOU KNOW?

One flock of passenger pigeons was estimated to contain over two billion birds. Eyewitnesses said it was like a cloud blocking out the sun.

MILK ON TAP

Both mother and father pigeons produce a sort of 'milk' to feed to their young chicks. This is like the milk human mothers feed to their babies. It helps the baby pigeons get enough energy and nutrients to grow fast.

THE CROWNED PIGEONS OF NEW GUINEA ARE AS BIG AS LARGE CHICKENS.

Some sheep-shearers can clip a lamb in less than a minute.

EYES ON THE SIDE OF THE HEAD WATCH FOR DANGER ALL AROUND.

SHEEP USUALLY HAVE SHORT TAILS.

FLAT CHEEK TEETH GRIND UP THE GRASSES THE SHEEP EATS.

THE WOOLLY COAT HELPS TO KEEP THE SHEEP WARM.

THERE ARE MORE SHEEP THAN PEOPLE IN AUSTRALIA.

SHEEP

Farmers keep sheep for their wool, but also for their meat, milk and skins. There are over 200 different types of domestic sheep, varying in size, colour, and the length and quality of their fleeces. Male sheep are called rams. They can be distinguished from females by their longer horns.

FURRY FLOCK

Sheep are timid animals that live on farms in large groups called flocks. Farm sheep have a much thicker coat than wild sheep. Their coat is called a fleece and it helps to keep them warm.

HAIR CUT

Sheep on farms do not shed their winter coat in the spring, like wild sheep do. So they have to have their wool cut off. This is called being sheared.

TERRIFIC TAIL

Some sheep have very fat tails. They live in hot or cold places and can use this store of fat to give them energy when food is hard to find.

COW

We keep cattle on farms to provide us with milk, meat and leather. From milk, we get cheese, butter and yoghurt. Cows usually live in herds and feed on grasses, using their teeth to pull it up by its roots.

MILK BAR

Cows make lots of tasty milk for their calves to drink. The milk is stored in the udders between their back legs. People milk cows by hand or with machines, which pull and squeeze the cows' teats to make the milk come out.

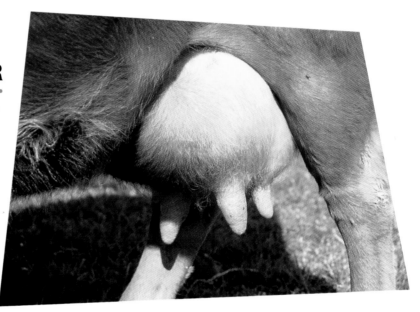

BULL OR COW?

Male cattle like this one are called bulls and females are called cows. Both bulls and cows can have horns. Wild bulls use their horns to compete for cows in the herd and both bulls and cows use their horns for defence.

THEIR EARS CAN TURN TOWARDS SOUNDS TO HEAR THEM MORE CLEARLY.

DOMESTIC CATTLE, INCLUDING SPANISH FIGHTING BULLS, CANNOT SEE THE COLOUR RED.

CHEWING THE CUD

Cattle have large stomachs with four parts, called chambers. In chambers 1 and 2, food is broken down by bacteria into pulp, or cud. The cattle cough up the cud and chew it again before it goes to chambers 3 and 4. This long process helps the cattle to get as much goodness as possible out of their food.

THE LONG BODY MAKES ROOM FOR THEIR LARGE STOMACH.

THE TAIL HAS A HAIRY TUFT AT THE END TO WHISK AWAY THE FLIES.

THEY HAVE LOTS OF TEETH AT THE BACK OF THE JAW TO CHEW GRASSES.

THERE ARE TWO TOES ON EACH FOOT SO THE HOOF LOOKS AS IF IT IS SPLIT INTO TWO.

DID YOU KNOW?

There are over 220 million dairy cows in the world, producing about 480 million tonnes of milk each year.

ZEBU CATTLE ARE SACRED TO THE HINDU PEOPLE AND ROAM FREELY ON THE STREETS OF INDIA.

EARS CAN BE LIFTED TO LISTEN TO SOUNDS.

WHITER THAN WHITE

Sheepdogs are usually a light colour or have large patches of white in their coats. This helps them to be seen more easily by the shepherd in bad weather or in the dark.

A WET NOSE HELPS THE DOG TO PICK UP SMELLS FROM ITS SURROUNDINGS.

DID YOU KNOW?

Sheepdogs will herd ducks, geese and even children because they have such a strong instinct to do so!

LARGE LUNGS AND STRONG MUSCLES HELP THE DOG RUN FAST.

IN THE OLDEN DAYS, SHEPHERDS USED WHITE DOGS TO TELL THEM APART FROM WOLVES.

SHEEPDOG

Sheepdogs are intelligent, lively and agile. They easily learn and respond to human commands. They have strong, muscular bodies and are able to run with short bursts of high speed. There are many different breeds of sheepdog, including the shepherd's favourite, the border collie.

TOP DOG

Herding sheep is not an easy task. A well-trained sheepdog listens carefully to its owner's every call and whistle and keeps a watchful eye out for any hand signals they may give. Some sheepdogs control their sheep with a silent stare. Others drive their flock by barking, circling and nipping at their heels.

TRUSTY FRIEND

A shepherd relies on his faithful sheepdog to help him protect his sheep, keep the flock together and make them move from place to place.

A GOOD SENSE OF SMELL HELPS THE DOG TO SNIFF OUT LAMBS OR SHEEP BURIED IN THE SNOW.

ROOSTER

A rooster is a male chicken, sometimes known as a cock or cockerel. Many people keep chickens for their meat or eggs. Free-range chickens wander about in farmyards or fields. Other chickens are kept in tiny cages indoors on battery farms.

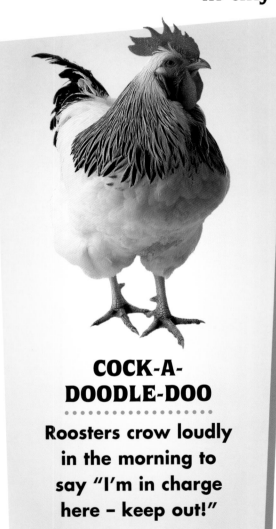

COCK-A-DOODLE-DOO

Roosters crow loudly in the morning to say "I'm in charge here – keep out!"

HAY HAY

Roosters do not lay eggs. They often live in barns which are covered in hay. The hay acts as a bed for them to sleep on in the same way that you snuggle up in your bed.

RULING THE ROOST

Roosters strut around fearlessly, showing off their colourful feathers, combs and wattles to the females. Female chickens are quieter and less colourful than the males. They are called hens.

IN THE OLDEN DAYS, ROOSTERS USED TO WAKE UP SOLDIERS FOR BATTLE AT DAWN.

THESE FLAPS OF SKIN ARE CALLED WATTLES.

ROOSTERS OFTEN HAVE LONG TAIL FEATHERS TO IMPRESS THE HENS.

THEIR WINGS ARE NOT VERY GOOD FOR FLYING.

SHARP CLAWS ARE USED TO SCRATCH IN THE DIRT FOR FOOD.

DID YOU KNOW?

There are more chickens than people in the world – over 8,000 million of them!

A CHAMPION CHICKEN ONCE LAID 353 EGGS IN A YEAR.

The stomach of a Vietnamese pot-bellied pig is so low that it touches the ground.

POWERFUL, AGILE BODIES HAVE PLENTY OF FAT AND MUSCLES.

LARGE EARS HELP PIGS TO HEAR WELL.

THERE ARE FOUR TOES ON EACH FOOT.

THE SNOUT IS FLAT AT THE TIP WITH HUGE NOSTRILS.

PIGS ARE RELATED TO HIPPOPOTAMUSES!

PIG

Pigs are intelligent animals with a very good sense of hearing and smell. They are kept on farms to provide pork, bacon and ham – in fact, they provide more meat around the world than any other animal. Pigs are also popular as pets.

BIG NOSE

Pigs use their long, sensitive snouts to sniff for food, such as roots and worms, in the soil. Some French farmers train their pigs to sniff out truffles hidden underground. (Truffles are mushrooms, not chocolates!)

STRIPES RULE OK

The biggest wild pig is the wild boar. Young wild boars have stripy coats, which help to camouflage them from enemies. The adults have a plain brown coat.

PIGLET HEAVEN

A female pig is called a sow. She can have about 22 piglets in a year. The piglets feed on their mother's milk.

PIGS ARE NOISY ANIMALS THAT GRUNT, CHIRRUP AND SQUEAK AT EACH OTHER.

SHIRE HORSE

Large, strong shire horses are surprisingly quiet and gentle animals, which are easy to control. They worked on farms a lot in the past. They are called shire horses because they were bred in the shires of Lincoln, Leicester, Derby and Stafford.

HORSES AT WORK

In northern Europe, the soils are damp and full of sticky clay, so the farm horses needed to be strong and powerful. The padded horse collar allowed the horse to take the weight on its strong shoulders and use its full power.

PULLING THE PLOUGH

Before tractors were invented, shire horses used to pull the ploughs that prepared the soil for planting crops. Some still work like this today. Horses do not pollute the air or squash the soil flat like a tractor.

POWER PAIR

Shire horses used to pull heavy carts full of beer barrels through city streets to deliver beer. Today, their carts are more likely to be full of tourists than beer barrels.

SHIRE HORSES WERE DEVELOPED FROM ENGLAND'S MEDIEVAL WAR HORSE, THE GREAT HORSE.

The only animal stronger than a shire horse is an elephant! A fully grown shire horse weighs over a tonne and is taller than a person.

DID YOU KNOW?

THEY HAVE BROAD HEADS WITH LARGE KIND EYES.

THEY HAVE WIDE BODIES, WITH A SHORT, BROAD BACK.

STRONG LEG MUSCLES GIVE POWER.

THEY HAVE BIG, STRONG CHESTS.

THEIR LARGE, ROUND HOOVES ARE COVERED WITH LONG, STRAIGHT, SILKY HAIRS.

Five goats take a year to grow enough wool to make one Cashmere sweater!

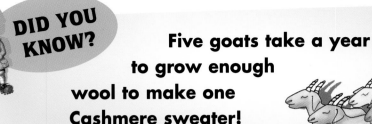

A GOAT'S TAIL USUALLY STANDS UP.

LARGE EARS LISTEN OUT FOR DANGER.

GOATS HAVE SEVERAL STOMACHS AND CHEW THEIR FOOD AT LEAST TWICE.

BEST FLEECE

Angora goats grow fine, silky wool called mohair. The word mohair comes from an Arabic word meaning 'best fleece'. Several breeds of goat produce Cashmere wool, including the Cashmere goat itself.

MALE GOATS ARE CALLED BILLIES OR RAMS, FEMALE GOATS ARE CALLED NANNIES OR DOES.

GOAT

Goats are friendly, inquisitive animals that can eat almost anything! even metal. Their tough lips allow them to feed on thorny bushes and spiky grasses. Goats provide people with milk, meat and wool.

WOOLLY JUMPER

Many goats on farms have been bred for their long woolly coats or large horns. In the wild, goats live in cold mountainous places so the 'woolly jumpers' help to keep them warm. They use their horns to fight for mates.

HORNS GROW OUT OF THE TOP OF THE HEAD.

PARTY TRICKS

Goats are brilliant at climbing trees in search of food. They can also undo gates, destroy fences and chew their way through ropes and tethers.

YOUNG GOATS, CALLED KIDS, CAN STAND UP SOON AFTER THEY ARE BORN.

MONITOR LIZARD

Monitor lizards are a small family of rather large lizards, with long necks, strong legs and long, muscular tails. They are big enough to catch other reptiles, birds and mammals and usually swallow their prey whole, like a snake.

THERE BE DRAGONS!

The largest lizard in the world is the Komodo dragon. It can grow up to three metres long and kill animals as large as pigs and small deer. Sometimes, it even attacks people. A Komodo dragon is a good swimmer and can also climb trees.

A LONG, NARROW HEAD WITH A POINTED SNOUT.

SHARP, FANG-LIKE TEETH AND FORKED TONGUE

TONGUE TASTER

Most lizards have fleshy pink tongues but monitor lizards have thin, forked tongues, like snakes. All lizards use their tongues to taste and to smell.

THE COMMON ASIATIC MONITOR CAN STAY UNDERWATER FOR UP TO AN HOUR.

DID YOU KNOW?

A 46 kg Komodo dragon once ate a whole 41 kg pig in one meal.

AT HOME

Monitors are daytime lizards that live in all sorts of places on land, from deserts and grasslands to forests, riverbanks and swamps. They are common in Australia. One monitor, called the Common Asiatic monitor, has even been seen swimming far out to sea.

THE TAIL IS LONG AND STRONG AND IS SOMETIMES USED AS A WEAPON.

FIVE STRONG TOES ARE ARMED WITH SHARP CLAWS.

IT HAS SCALY, WATERPROOF SKIN.

Geckos wear glasses! Instead of eyelids, they have a large, see-through spectacle over each eye. They can't blink to clean their spectacles but may clean them with their tongue instead.

SUCKER TOES

A gecko's toe pads are ridges covered with millions of tiny hairs. These help the gecko to grip tiny bumps and dips in a surface so it can walk up and down walls and even upside down across ceilings!

A TOUGH, WATERPROOF, SCALY SKIN IS SHED MONTHLY.

SUCKER PADS HELP TO GRIP SURFACES.

FAT STORED IN THE TAIL IS USED FOR ENERGY WHEN FOOD IS SCARCE.

A GECKO CAN CLING TO GLASS SO TIGHTLY THAT PULLING IT OFF WILL BREAK THE GLASS.

GECKO

A gecko is a type of lizard that lives in hot countries and comes out to hunt for insects at night. Geckos have good hearing and make a variety of chirping, clicking and barking noises to attract a mate or warn other geckos to keep out of their patch.

LARGE EYES WATCH FOR PREY AND DANGER.

GOOD LUCK CHARM

People like to hear the sound of geckos in their bedrooms at night because they catch insects, such as mosquitoes, which might bite or spread disease. Geckos are the only reptiles with a true voice, rather than just a hiss.

GOODBYE TAIL

If they are attacked, geckos can shed their tail and run away. Their tail wriggles away on the ground, which confuses the enemy long enough for the lizard to make good its escape. The gecko grows a new tail to replace the old one.

HOUSE GECKOS IN MALAYSIA ARE CALLED 'DUP-DUPS' BECAUSE OF THE SOUNDS THEY MAKE.

CHAMELEON

Chameleons are lizards that live in the hot forests of Africa and Madagascar. They climb slowly through the trees, clinging on tightly with their special gripping tails. Male chameleons fight each other to claim their own patch of forest.

ALL-SEEING EYES

The eyes of a chameleon can swivel in all directions to look for danger or possible meals. One eye can also look in a different direction from the other eye.

NEW CLOTHES

Chameleons are usually well camouflaged. They can change colour completely in just a few minutes because of changes in light, temperature and even mood, such as being angry or frightened.

TERRIFIC TONGUE

To catch insects and spiders, a chameleon shoots out its long tongue like a catapult. The prey is trapped on the swollen tip of the tongue, which is sticky, like strong glue. A chameleon flicks its tongue in and out in the blink of an eye, so its victim is taken by surprise and has no chance to escape.

SOME MALE CHAMELEONS USE THEIR HORNS TO FIGHT OTHER MALES.

EYES ARE ON TURRETS AND TURN AROUND EASILY.

ITS SKIN IS CAMOUFLAGED TO MATCH ITS SURROUNDINGS.

ITS SCALY SKIN IS TOUGH AND WATERPROOF.

ITS TAIL CURLS ROUND BRANCHES FOR BALANCE.

DID YOU KNOW?

A chameleon's tongue is often longer than its body and tail combined!

A CHAMELEON'S TONGUE CAN BE SHOT OUT AND PULLED BACK IN AS LITTLE AS 0.04 SECONDS!

DID YOU KNOW?

The pancake tortoise has a shell as flat as a pancake! This helps it to squeeze into the narrow spaces between rocks to escape enemies.

THE HIGH, DOMED SHELL GOES RIGHT ROUND THE BODY.

STRONG, THICK LEGS SUPPORT THE WEIGHT OF THE SHELL.

A TORTOISE HAS A REPTILE'S SCALY SKIN.

LONG, SHARP CLAWS GRIP SURFACES AND PULL THE TORTOISE ALONG.

TORTOISES CAN LIVE FOR 150 YEARS OR MORE!

TORTOISE

Tortoises are the only reptiles with hard, bony shells covering their soft bodies like a suit of armour, protecting the tortoise from enemies and bad weather.

ARMOUR PLATING

A tortoise's strong shell is made of two parts - the dome is called the carapace and the flat underbelly is called the plastron. The shell is made from bony plates covered by large scales called scutes, made of the same material as your fingernails.

TOOTHLESS WONDER

Tortoises do not have teeth. Instead they use their sharp jaws to hold and cut up their food. Adult tortoises move too slowly to catch prey, so they eat flowers, fruit and plants.

DISAPPEARING TRICK

Many tortoises can pull their head and legs back inside their shell, making it hard for enemies to eat them.

TORTOISES GO TO SLEEP FOR MONTHS AT A TIME WHEN IT GETS TOO HOT OR TOO COLD.

BOA

Boas are snakes that kill their prey by squeezing it to death. There are about 39 different kinds, many of which live in Central and South America. Many boas have a slender body and a long tail but large anacondas are thick and heavy snakes.

GIANT SNAKES

Most boas are not enormous, but some grow very large indeed. Boa constrictors grow three to five metres long, while green anacondas grow at least nine metres long. Imagine holding a snake this size!

A TIGHT SQUEEZE

Boas seize animals with their sharp teeth and wrap their bodies around their victims. Slowly they squeeze tighter and tighter

until the victims cannot breathe any more. Then the boa swallows its prey whole – usually head-first so it slides down more easily.

HOT LIPS

Many boas have heat holes along their lips. These holes can sense the hot bodies of the boa's prey, which helps these snakes to hunt in the dark.

GREEN ANACONDAS ARE THE HEAVIEST SNAKES IN THE WORLD AND WEIGH UP TO 227KG.

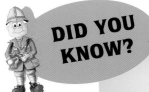

DID YOU KNOW?

Boas give birth to their young - up to 100 of them at a time!

THE BOA'S SCALES ARE CAMOUFLAGED TO HIDE FROM ITS PREY.

RIDGES ON THE BELLY SCALES HELP THE BOA TO GRIP TREE BRANCHES.

ITS POINTED HEAD SLIDES EASILY THROUGH BRANCHES.

THIS EMERALD GREEN TREE BOA HANGS FROM TREE BRANCHES AND SEIZES BIRDS AS THEY FLY PAST.

EMERALD TREE BOAS ARE ORANGE, YELLOW OR PINK WHEN THEY ARE BORN, NOT GREEN.

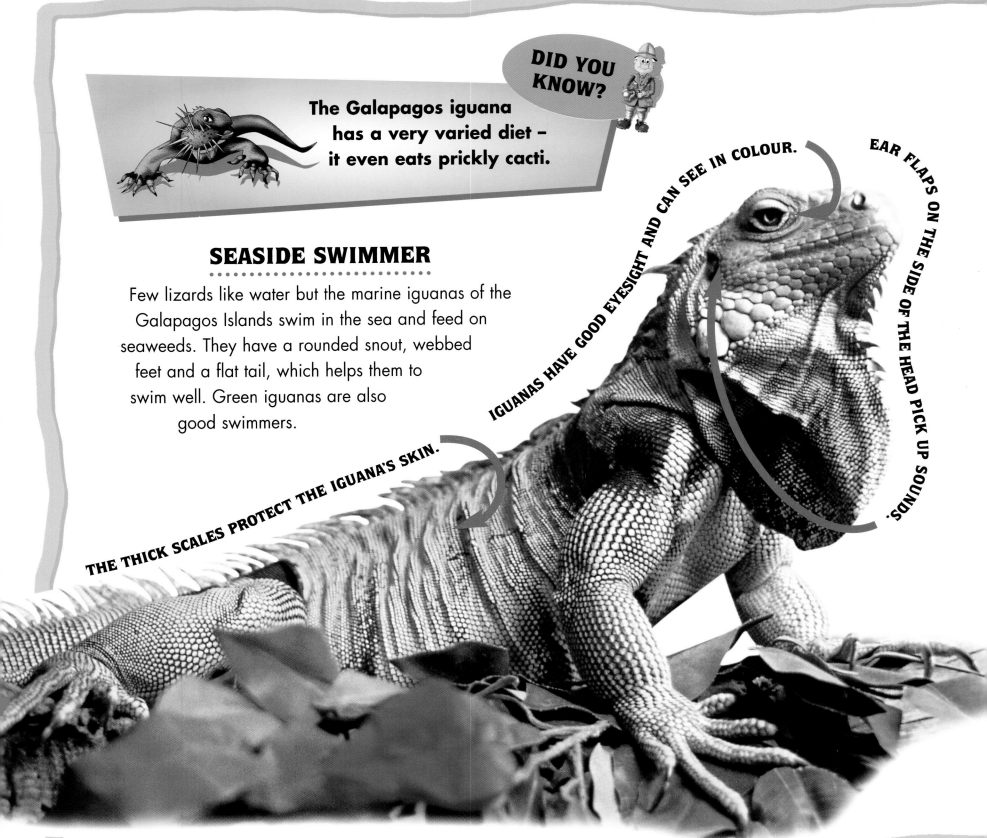

The Galapagos iguana has a very varied diet – it even eats prickly cacti.

SEASIDE SWIMMER

Few lizards like water but the marine iguanas of the Galapagos Islands swim in the sea and feed on seaweeds. They have a rounded snout, webbed feet and a flat tail, which helps them to swim well. Green iguanas are also good swimmers.

IGUANAS HAVE GOOD EYESIGHT AND CAN SEE IN COLOUR.

EAR FLAPS ON THE SIDE OF THE HEAD PICK UP SOUNDS.

THE THICK SCALES PROTECT THE IGUANA'S SKIN.

 AN IGUANA CALLED THE BASILISK CAN WALK ON WATER – IT HAS TO MOVE VERY FAST!

IGUANA

This large family of lizards lives mostly in hot parts of the Americas. Iguanas come out during the daytime and most of them have special displays to defend their living space or attract a mate. Small iguanas eat insects or other small animals but bigger iguanas eat plants.

CLIMB, RUN AND BURROW

Green iguanas are good at climbing trees. Their long toes and sharp claws help them to grip tree trunks and branches. Other iguanas, such as the desert iguana and the basilisk, can run on their back legs. The fringe-toed lizard can burrow through loose sand, helped by the fringe of scales on its toes.

SHOWING OFF

Many male iguanas show off to rival males or females. They do things like bobbing up and down, moving their crests or throat flaps, and snapping their tails. These displays are instead of real fights.

THE HORNED LIZARD CAN SPRAY BLOOD FROM ITS EYES TO FRIGHTEN ENEMIES AWAY.

PYTHON

Pythons are snakes that come from Africa, Asia and Australasia. They kill their prey by squeezing, or constricting, and are not poisonous snakes. Some of the pythons are giant-sized, but there are small pythons too. There are about 27 different kinds.

HEAT HOLES

Nearly all pythons have a row of holes along the mouth, which are sensitive to heat. Pythons may use their heat holes to sense the body heat of their prey, such as rats or birds. This helps them to find their prey in the dark.

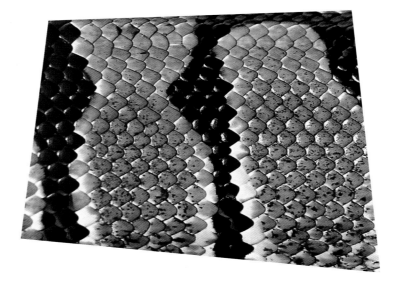

STRETCHY ARMOUR

A snake's scales are extra-thick pieces of skin, made of the same stuff as your fingernails and hair. They work like a suit of armour to protect the snake's body as it slithers about. They also allow the skin to stretch as the snake moves or feeds.

ADULT SNAKES SHED THEIR SKIN UP TO SIX TIMES A YEAR.

EGGY SNAKES

One of the ways in which pythons are different from boas is that pythons lay eggs, whereas boas give birth to their young. Some pythons coil around their eggs to guard them. Female Indian pythons may 'shiver' to help keep their eggs warm.

DID YOU KNOW?

The reticulated python could stretch all the way from the ground to the roof of a three-storey house! It grows up to 10 metres long and is probably the longest snake in the world.

THE THIN PART AT THE END OF A SNAKE'S BODY IS ITS TAIL.

PYTHONS HAVE A LARGE, THICK, ROUND BODY.

HOLES ALONG THE EDGES OF THE MOUTH SENSE THE HEAT FROM PREY.

THIS ROYAL PYTHON IS ALSO CALLED THE BALL PYTHON BECAUSE IT CURLS INTO A BALL WHEN IT IS ALARMED.

LAZY LIONS

Lions spend up to 20 hours a day sleeping and resting. After a big meal, they may laze around for up to three days while their food goes down.

DID YOU KNOW?

A male lion can eat 23 kg of food at one sitting, which is the same as a person eating 16 steaks in one meal!

LARGE EYES HELP LIONS TO HUNT IN THE DARK.

A MUSCULAR BODY FOR CATCHING AND KILLING PREY.

WHISKERS ARE FOR FEELING OBJECTS IN THE DARK.

ONLY ONE IN FIVE LION HUNTS ENDS IN A KILL.

LION

Lions are the largest meat-eaters in Africa. They live in groups called prides. Female lions, called lionesses, catch food for the pride while the male lions protect the pride from rival males and hyenas.

PADDY PAWS

Like a pet cat, a lion can pull in its claws so they stay sharp. When a lion attacks its prey, it flicks out its claws. The huge, spiky paws help to drag the prey to the ground, so the lion can kill it with a suffocating bite.

MAGNIFICENT MANE

A male lion has a hairy mane to make him look bigger and more frightening to enemies. The mane also protects his neck and back during a fight.

LIONS ARE POWERFUL ENOUGH TO HUNT ANIMALS AS LARGE AS HIPPOS.

WOLF

Wolves are fierce, intelligent hunters that live in packs of between eight and twenty wolves. The oldest male and female wolf usually lead the pack. They are the only wolves to mate and have cubs.

HUNTING MACHINE

Wolves have strong bodies and long, powerful legs for chasing their prey. They are agile animals that can keep running for long distances of up to ten kilometres.

HELPFUL HUNTERS

By hunting together, wolves can kill animals that are much bigger than they are, such as a musk ox or moose. The wolves chase their prey until it gets tired, then move in to bite the animal to death.

HORRIBLE HOWLS

Wolves howl to keep in touch with each other or to warn other wolves to keep out of their area. If one wolf howls, the others usually join in. They can be heard as far as ten kilometres away.

WOLVES CAN RUN AT SPEEDS OF UP TO 65 KM/H.

DID YOU KNOW?

Wolves can pull as many as 17 different faces.

FUR IN THE EARS TRAPS BODY HEAT

THICK FUR COAT HELPS THE WOLF TO KEEP WARM.

POWERFUL JAWS HAVE 42 SHARP TEETH FOR KILLING PREY.

IT WALKS OR RUNS ON ITS TOES TO MOVE FASTER.

A WOLF'S TEETH HAVE TWICE THE CRUSHING POWER OF A GERMAN SHEPHERD DOG.

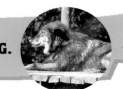

FRIENDLY CROCS

Adult crocodiles sometimes gather together in groups to bask in the sun, share food, find a mate or build nests. Young crocodiles often stay together in groups called pods, because there is safety in numbers. If they are in danger, they call loudly to the adults for help.

A big crocodile sometimes has to wait two years for a meal! It uses the fat stored in its tail and other parts of its body to give it the energy to survive.

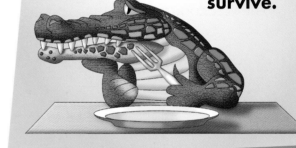

CROCODILES ARE THE CLEVEREST REPTILES AND CAN LEARN THINGS.

TOUGH, SCALY SKIN IS FOR PROTECTION AND CAMOUFLAGE.

CROCODILES WERE ALIVE IN THE DAYS OF THE DINOSAURS...

CROCODILE

Crocodiles are fierce predators that lurk in the water, waiting to snap up prey in their enormous jaws. The biggest ones catch animals as large as cattle, zebra and horses. Crocodiles come onto land to sunbathe, nest and lay their eggs.

BABY CARRIER

A mother crocodile gently picks up her babies in her mouth and carries them from their nest to the water. This helps to keep them safe from enemies. The babies stay close to their mother for the first few weeks of their life, often resting in safety on her broad back.

A LONG SNOUT IS FULL OF SHARP SPIKY TEETH.

BIG MOUTH

A crocodile's jaws are so strong that, when they snap shut, they can crush an animal's bones. However, the muscles that open the crocodile's jaw are so weak that an elastic band can hold its mouth closed.

MOSQUITO

Female mosquitoes bite people and other animals because most of them need a meal of blood before their eggs can develop. Female mosquitoes are dangerous because they spread diseases such as malaria and yellow fever as they feed.

DANGER MOUTH

A female mosquito makes a tiny hole in her victim's skin with six mouthparts that are like sharp needles. Then she sucks up a meal of blood. The mosquito pumps saliva into the wound to stop the victim's blood from clotting and keep it flowing freely.

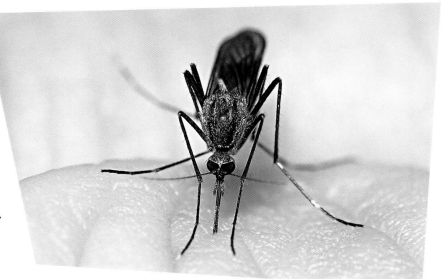

SUPER SNORKEL

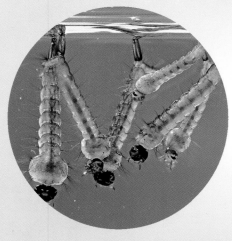

Mosquito eggs hatch into larvae, which hang upside down from the surface of the water. They take in oxygen from the air through a 'snorkel' at the rear end of the body.

MALE MOSQUITOES DO NOT BITE. THEY FEED FROM PLANTS.

SLEEPLESS NIGHTS

The high-pitched whine of a mosquito that keeps us awake at night is a mating call made by the wings of the female. A male mosquito picks up the sound with the fine hairs on his antennae.

DID YOU KNOW?

Mosquitoes kill more people every year than any other creature!

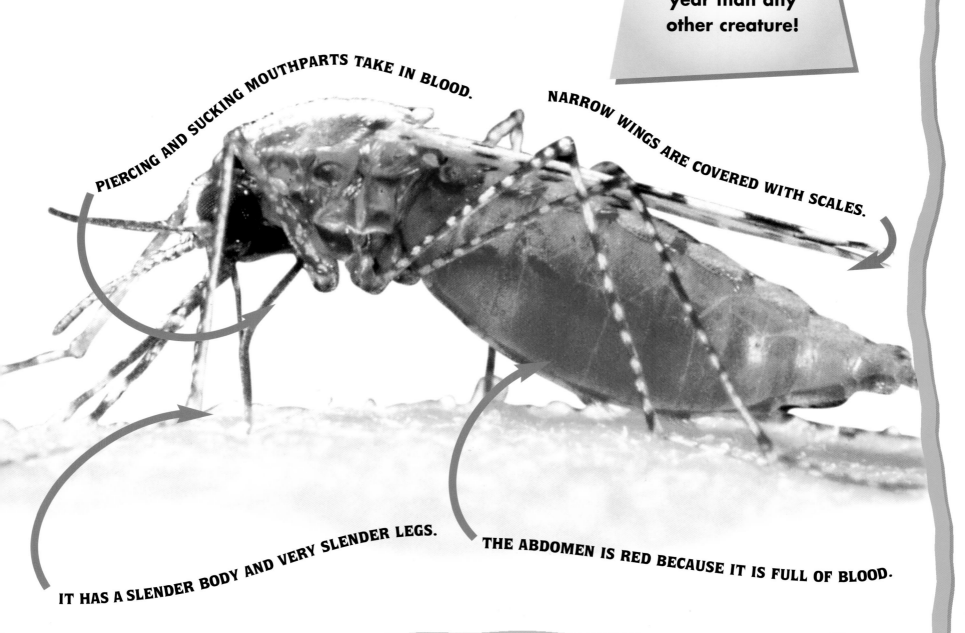

PIERCING AND SUCKING MOUTHPARTS TAKE IN BLOOD.

NARROW WINGS ARE COVERED WITH SCALES.

IT HAS A SLENDER BODY AND VERY SLENDER LEGS.

THE ABDOMEN IS RED BECAUSE IT IS FULL OF BLOOD.

FEMALE MOSQUITOES MATE ONLY ONCE, THEN THEY LAY HUNDREDS OF EGGS.

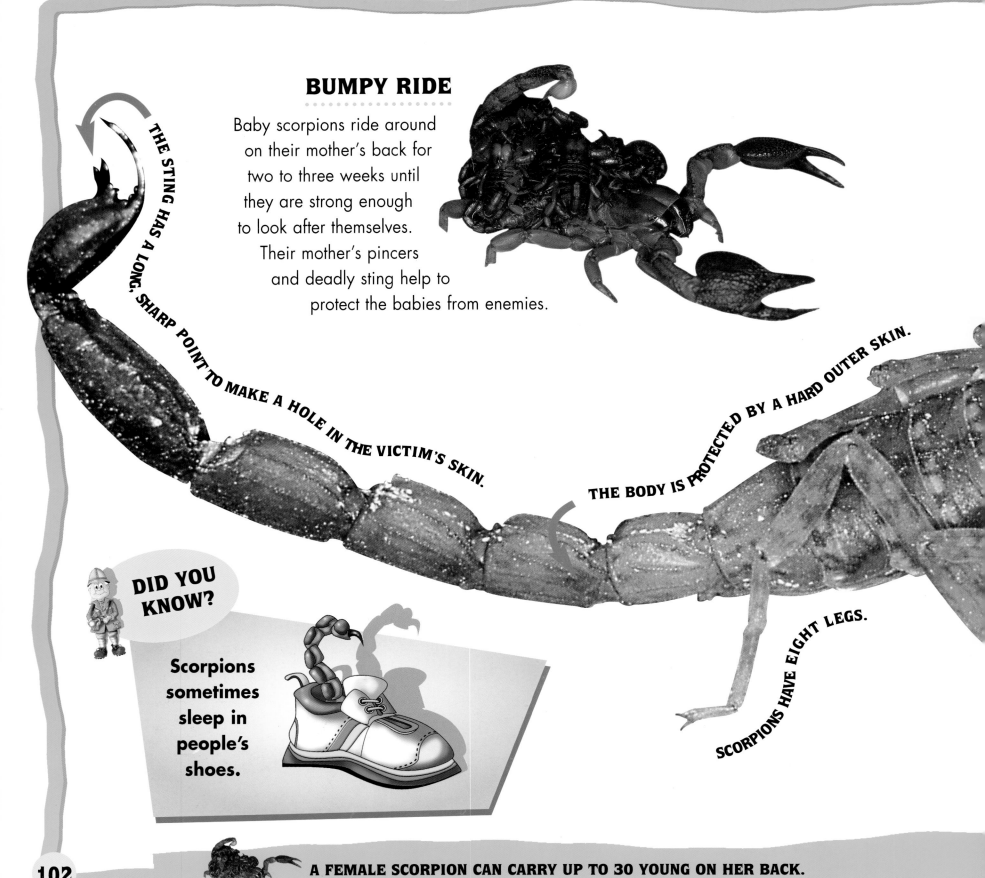

BUMPY RIDE

Baby scorpions ride around on their mother's back for two to three weeks until they are strong enough to look after themselves. Their mother's pincers and deadly sting help to protect the babies from enemies.

THE STING HAS A LONG, SHARP POINT TO MAKE A HOLE IN THE VICTIM'S SKIN.

THE BODY IS PROTECTED BY A HARD OUTER SKIN.

SCORPIONS HAVE EIGHT LEGS.

DID YOU KNOW?

Scorpions sometimes sleep in people's shoes.

A FEMALE SCORPION CAN CARRY UP TO 30 YOUNG ON HER BACK.

SCORPION

Scorpions are small animals with eight legs, big pincers and a sting in the tail. They sting to protect themselves and to kill prey. Most scorpions are not dangerous to people. They live mainly in warm places and come out at night to hunt.

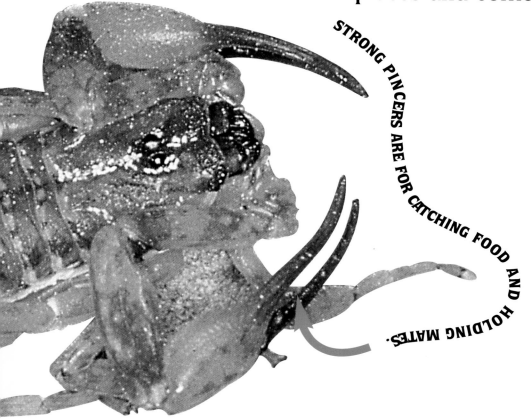

STRONG PINCERS ARE FOR CATCHING FOOD AND HOLDING MATES.

POWERFUL PINCERS

Scorpions catch and hold food in their strong pincers. They only sting their prey if it fights back fiercely. Male and female scorpions also hold each other by their pincers during their courtship dance.

STING IN THE TAIL

A scorpion's sting is a sharp spine at the end of its long tail. This spine injects poison into enemies or prey so the victim cannot move.

SCORPIONS CAN KILL ANIMALS AS LARGE AS LIZARDS, SOME CAN EVEN KILL HUMANS.

PUFFERFISH

Pufferfish can puff up their bodies with air or water so they look much bigger than they really are. Many pufferfish have dangerous poisons inside their bodies and people can die if they eat them. In Japan, chefs carefully clean the fish to remove the poison so that the fish is safe to eat.

KEEP AWAY!

The lionfish has very poisonous spines and its stripy colours warn enemies to leave it alone. Some pufferfish have spines that stick out like a porcupine's spines when they puff themselves up into a ball shape.

PARROT BEAK

The pufferfish's teeth are stuck together so they look rather like a bird's beak. It feeds mainly on animals with hard shells, such as sea urchins, shellfish and crabs.

PRICKLY MOUTHFUL

This pufferfish is a normal size, but the one on the next page looks a lot bigger! It is trying to scare off an enemy and make itself hard for the enemy to swallow.

THERE ARE ABOUT 90 DIFFERENT KINDS OF PUFFERFISH.

IT HAS EYES ON THE SIDES OF THE HEAD.

DID YOU KNOW?

The flesh of a pufferfish, called fugu, is served as a very special meal in Japan. Eating comes with risks ... A few people die each year after eating fugu!

THE PUFFERFISH LOOKS HUGE WHEN IT GULPS DOWN WATER OR A

WIDE TEETH LOOK RATHER LIKE A BE

THE LARGEST P

The teddy bear is named after the 26th president of the United States, Theodore 'Ted' Roosevelt. He refused to shoot a bear cub on a hunting trip and toy bears went on sale soon afterwards known as 'teddy's bears'.

MASSIVE SHOULDERS AND FRONT LEGS MAKE THE BEAR VERY STRONG

THE BEAR TO KEEP WARM.

A SENSITIVE NOSE IS USED FOR SNIFFING OUT FOOD.

...RING WINTER HIBERNATION.

AK.

SPINES STICK OUT WHEN THE FISH PUFFS ITSELF UP.

IR.

UFFERS GROW TO ABOUT 90 CENTIMETRES LONG.

THICK FUR HELPS TH

SOME BEARS SLEEP FOR FIVE AND A HALF MONTHS AT A TIME DUR

BEAR

Bears may look soft and cuddly, but they are big, strong animals with huge heads, long, pointed teeth and sharp claws. Bears use their teeth and claws to fight each other and to defend their young.

SLOTH BEAR

The sloth bear has long, black, shaggy fur, long, curved claws and a mobile snout. It uses its claws to break open ant hills, bees' nests and termite mounds. It forms a tube with its mouth and tongue to suck up its insect food.

CARING FOR CUBS

Female polar bears have to protect their cubs from adult male polar bears, which might try to kill them. The cubs stay with their mother for a year while they learn how to survive and hunt on their own.

TEMPER TANTRUM

If a bear is threatened, it puts on a terrifying display. It beats the ground or plants with its front feet. Then it stands up on its back legs to make itself look larger. While the bear does this, it snorts or barks and snaps its jaws together.

BEETLE

Like tiny army tanks, beetles have a tough outer case made from a pair of hard, tough wings. These wings protect them from injury and from drying out.

COLOUR CHANGE

A ladybird's bright colours warn enemies to leave them alone because they taste bitter. When ladybird (ladybug) grubs change into adults, their outside wings are soft and yellow. After a few hours, the wings harden and turn red and the black spots appear.

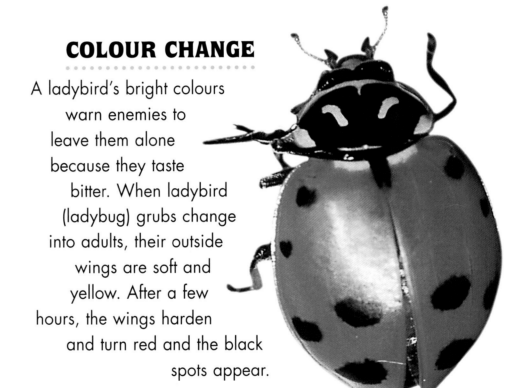

YUMMY DUNG

Female dung beetles roll up a ball of dung and lay eggs inside. When the beetle grub hatches out of the egg, it feeds on the dung.

GROWING UP

When beetles hatch out of their eggs, they look a bit like worms. They eat and grow bigger, then change their body shape completely and turn into adults. This is called complete metamorphosis.

LADYBIRDS SQUIRT HORRIBLE SMELLY LIQUID FROM THEIR KNEES IF ATTACKED BY ENEMIES.

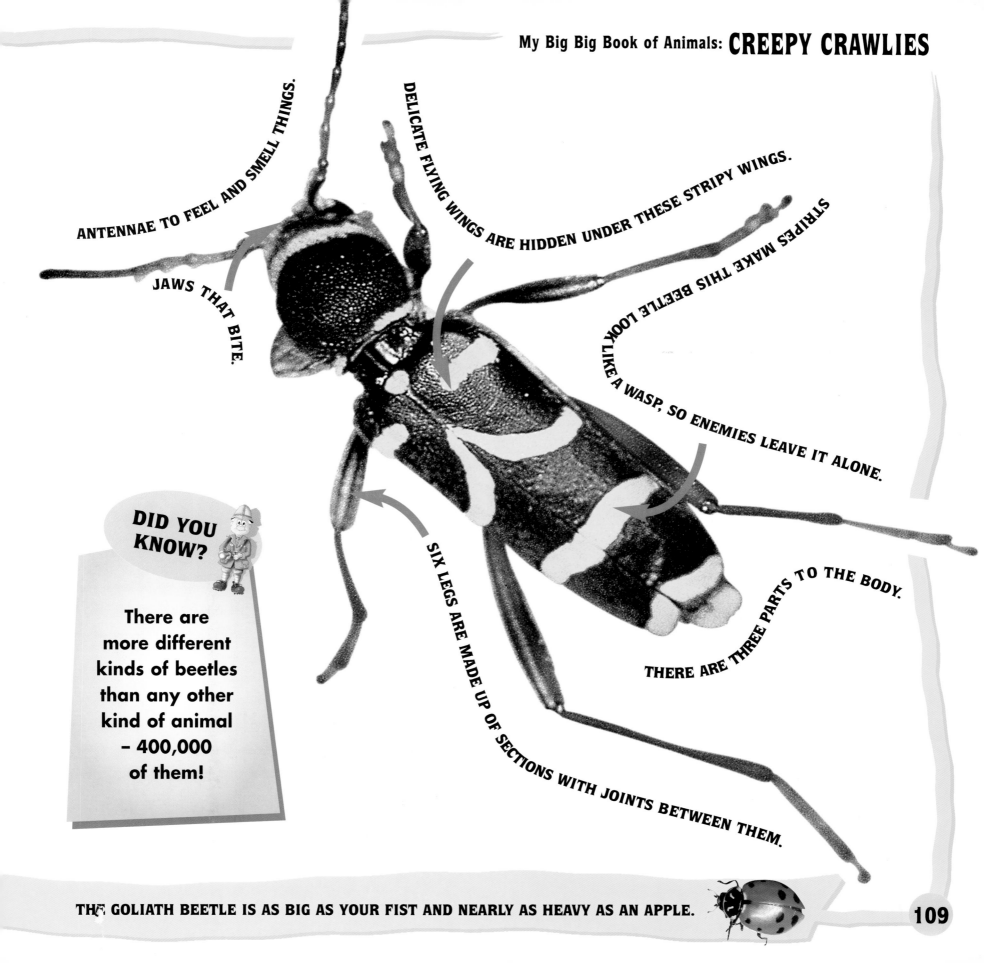

ANTENNAE TO FEEL AND SMELL THINGS.

DELICATE FLYING WINGS ARE HIDDEN UNDER THESE STRIPY WINGS.

STRIPES MAKE THIS BEETLE LOOK LIKE A WASP, SO ENEMIES LEAVE IT ALONE.

JAWS THAT BITE.

THERE ARE THREE PARTS TO THE BODY.

SIX LEGS ARE MADE UP OF SECTIONS WITH JOINTS BETWEEN THEM.

DID YOU KNOW?

There are more different kinds of beetles than any other kind of animal – 400,000 of them!

THE GOLIATH BEETLE IS AS BIG AS YOUR FIST AND NEARLY AS HEAVY AS AN APPLE.

Every autumn, monarch butterflies fly right across North America, from Canada to California or Mexico.

THE BUTTERFLY'S WINGS ARE BRIGHT COLOURS ON TOP.

THE ANTENNAE ARE SENSITIVE TO SCENT AND TOUCH.

LARGE EYES DETECT MOVEMENT AND COLOUR.

BUTTERFLIES HAVE TWO PAIRS OF WINGS.

THE ZEBRA BUTTERFLY GIVES OFF A NASTY SMELL TO PUT OFF ENEMIES.

BUTTERFLY

Most butterflies fly during the day and are brightly coloured. They use their colours to attract a mate or warn enemies that they are not good to eat. There are over 15,000 species of butterfly, the largest being the Queen Alexandra's Birdwing that is the size of a small bird.

SWALLOWTAILS

Swallowtail butterflies have large wings, often with a black and yellow pattern. Many of them have pointed tips to their back wings, like the forked tails of the birds called swallows, which is why they are called swallowtails. This citrus swallowtail does not have any wing tails.

THIS GATEKEEPER BUTTERFLY IS SO-CALLED BECAUSE IT LIVES NEAR GATES AT THE CORNERS OF FIELDS.

POWDER PUFFS

The wings of butterflies and moths are covered with thousands of tiny powdery scales. These scales overlap like the tiles on a roof. The colours of the wings come from pigments inside the scales or the way the scales reflect the light.

HIDDEN WINGS

When butterflies rest, they usually press their wings together and hold them up in the air. This shows only the underside of the wings, which are usually camouflaged.

BUTTERFLIES SUCK UP THEIR FOOD THROUGH A TUBE, WHICH IS RATHER LIKE A DRINKING STRAW.

111

MOTH

There are many more moths than butterflies. Most moths fly at night and are dark or pale colours. A few moths fly during the day and have bright colours. Moth wings tend to be longer and narrower than butterfly wings.

PERFUME TRAIL

Female moths release a special scent into the air to attract a male moth. Each kind of moth has a different scent. The male moth uses his antennae to smell the scent and follow the perfume trail to find a female.

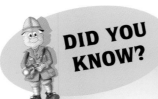

DID YOU KNOW?

Male long horn moths have antennae up to six times the length of their bodies.

BEWARE, POISON!

Burnet moth caterpillars take in poisons from the plants they eat and pass these poisons on to the adults. The adult moths are brightly coloured to warn predators that they are poisonous and not good to eat.

THE CATERPILLAR OF THE SOUTH AMERICAN WATER TIGER MOTH LIVES UNDERWATER AND CAN SWIM.

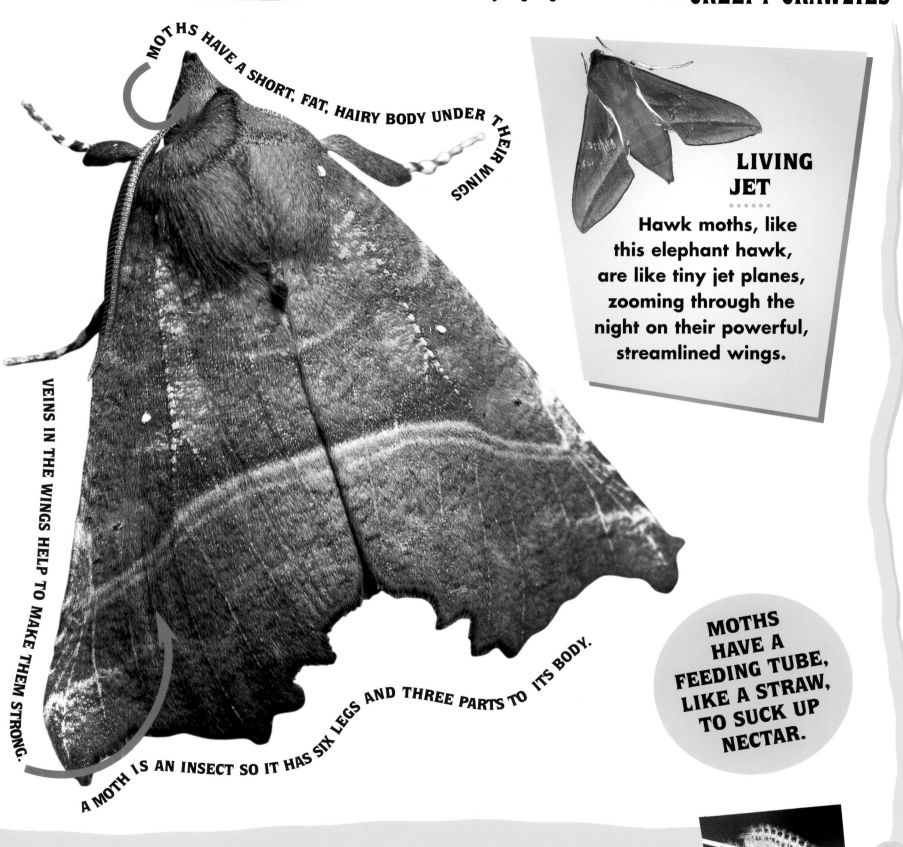

MOTHS HAVE A SHORT, FAT, HAIRY BODY UNDER THEIR WINGS

VEINS IN THE WINGS HELP TO MAKE THEM STRONG.

A MOTH IS AN INSECT SO IT HAS SIX LEGS AND THREE PARTS TO ITS BODY.

LIVING JET

Hawk moths, like this elephant hawk, are like tiny jet planes, zooming through the night on their powerful, streamlined wings.

MOTHS HAVE A FEEDING TUBE, LIKE A STRAW, TO SUCK UP NECTAR.

SILK COMES FROM THE COCOONS SPUN BY SILKMOTHS.

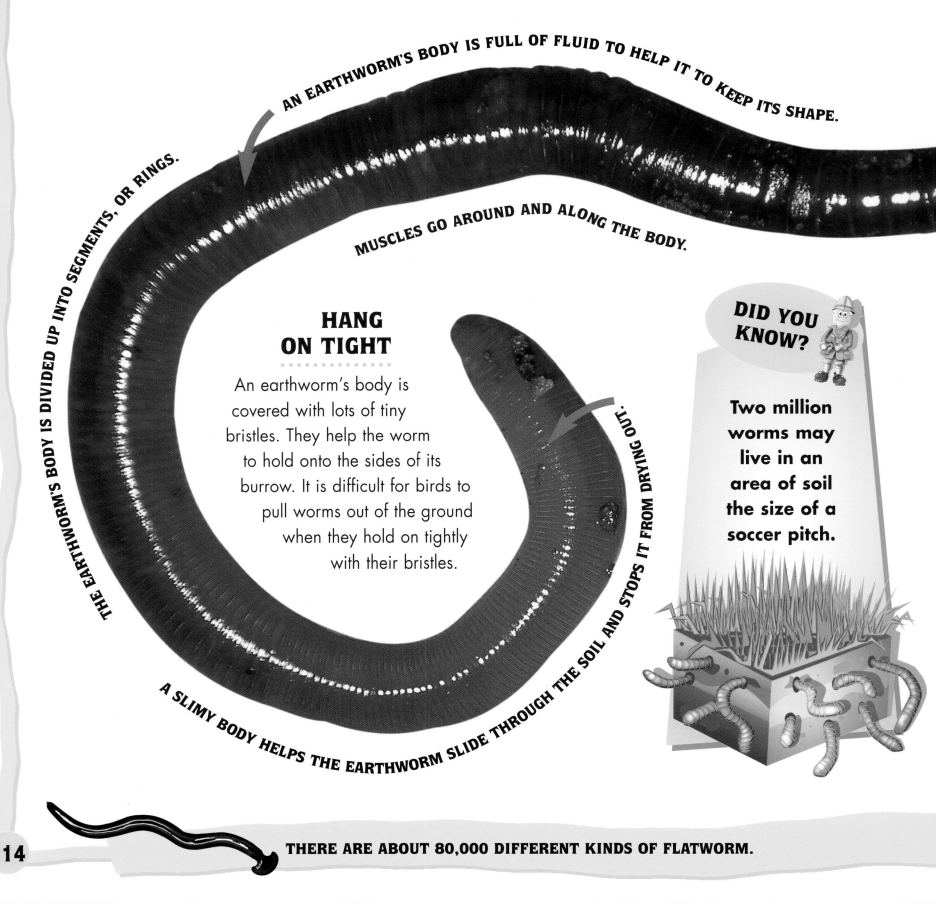

AN EARTHWORM'S BODY IS FULL OF FLUID TO HELP IT TO KEEP ITS SHAPE.

THE EARTHWORM'S BODY IS DIVIDED UP INTO SEGMENTS, OR RINGS.

MUSCLES GO AROUND AND ALONG THE BODY.

HANG ON TIGHT

An earthworm's body is covered with lots of tiny bristles. They help the worm to hold onto the sides of its burrow. It is difficult for birds to pull worms out of the ground when they hold on tightly with their bristles.

A SLIMY BODY HELPS THE EARTHWORM SLIDE THROUGH THE SOIL AND STOPS IT FROM DRYING OUT.

DID YOU KNOW?

Two million worms may live in an area of soil the size of a soccer pitch.

THERE ARE ABOUT 80,000 DIFFERENT KINDS OF FLATWORM.

WORM

There are millions of different kinds of worms, from ribbon worms and roundworms to flatworms and earthworms. The smallest worms are microscopic but the largest ones grow up to 12 metres long. They live in the soil, in the sea or in freshwater – some even live inside animals and plants.

FLATWORMS

Flatworms have no lungs so they breathe through their skin. Their flat bodies give them a large area for breathing.

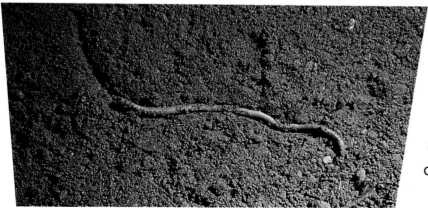

GARDENER'S FRIEND

Worms are good for the soil because their burrows let air and water into the soil and help to mix it up. Earthworms swallow soil and feed on the rotting plant and animal material it contains.

THERE ARE ABOUT 3,000 DIFFERENT KINDS OF EARTHWORM.

SPIDER

Spiders are hairy hunters that spin silk. They use their poisonous bite to kill or paralyse their prey or to defend themselves from enemies. Only about 30 kinds of spider are dangerous to people and there are over 35,000 different kinds!

EGG CARRIER

Female spiders spin a cocoon of silk around their eggs to protect them. Many carry their egg sac around with them. Most baby spiders look after themselves when they hatch, but some mothers guard and feed their young in a silk nest.

BIG EYES

Jumping spiders have extra large eyes to help them spot their prey. They can see in colour.

SPIDER IN THE BATH

The spiders that you sometimes find in the bath are usually male house spiders that fall in while looking for a mate. They cannot climb back up the slippery sides of the bath.

THE GOLIATH TARANTULA IS AS BIG AS A FRISBEE OR A DINNER PLATE.

SPIDERS HAVE TWO PARTS TO THE BODY – THE THORAX AND ABDOMEN.

THE ABDOMEN IS COVERED BY SOFT, STRETCHY SKIN.

HAIRS ARE USED TO TOUCH, TASTE AND HEAR.

THEY HAVE EIGHT HOLLOW LEGS WITH MANY JOINTS AND EIGHT EYES IN TWO OR THREE ROWS.

DID YOU KNOW?

Spider silk has more stretch than rubber and is stickier than sticky tape.

A JUMPING SPIDER'S TWO BIG EYES TOGETHER ARE BIGGER THAN ITS BRAIN.

DID YOU KNOW?

A snail can glide over a sharp knife without getting hurt because of its thick slime.

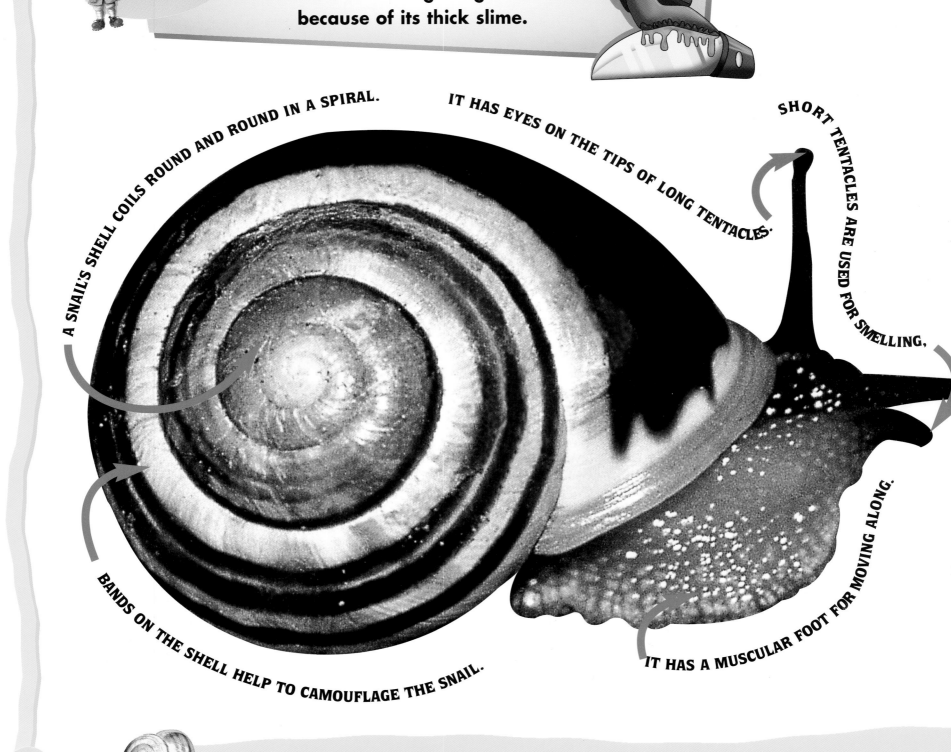

A SNAIL'S SHELL COILS ROUND AND ROUND IN A SPIRAL.

IT HAS EYES ON THE TIPS OF LONG TENTACLES.

SHORT TENTACLES ARE USED FOR SMELLING.

BANDS ON THE SHELL HELP TO CAMOUFLAGE THE SNAIL.

IT HAS A MUSCULAR FOOT FOR MOVING ALONG.

A GARDEN SNAIL WOULD TAKE FIVE DAYS TO TRAVEL A KILOMETRE – AT TOP SPEED.

SNAIL & SLUG

Snails and slugs are slow-moving animals with soft, slimy bodies. Snails have a shell but most slugs do not. There are over 72,000 different kinds, but most live in the seas and oceans.

NAIL FILE

On their tongue, snails have thousands of tiny, hook-shaped teeth called a radula. They use the radula like a nail file to scratch and scoop off bits of plants to eat. As the teeth wear down, new teeth grow to replace them.

BIGFOOT

Slugs and snails move along on a big, wide foot. Muscles in the foot move in waves to push the animal forwards. A gooey trail of slime oozes out of the foot to help it slide along more easily.

VANISHING TRICK

Snails can quickly pull their body right back inside their shell to escape danger or dry weather.

THE GIANT AFRICAN SNAIL HAS A SHELL ABOUT 20 CM LONG.

ANT

Ants are social insects that live together in large groups and help each other to survive. They 'talk' to each other using scent messages or by tapping each other with their antennae.

IN SOME FORESTS, LEAFCUTTER ANTS MAY EAT OVER 15% OF ALL THE LEAVES.

ANT GARDENERS

Leafcutter ants bite off pieces of leaf and carry them back to their underground nest. Here they use the leaves to make a compost for growing mushrooms, which they eat.

ANT CITY

Hundreds or thousands of ants live together in well-organised groups called colonies. The worker ants share out the different jobs, such as feeding and rearing the young, while soldier ants defend the nest. Only the queen ant lays eggs.

SOME ARMY ANTS TAKE YOUNG ANTS FROM OTHER NESTS AND USE THEM AS SLAVES.

ARMY ANTS

Tropical army ants march across the forest floor killing and eating other insects and any small animals that cannot run away fast enough. At night, the ants rest in a living nest made from the bodies of the ants with their legs locked together.

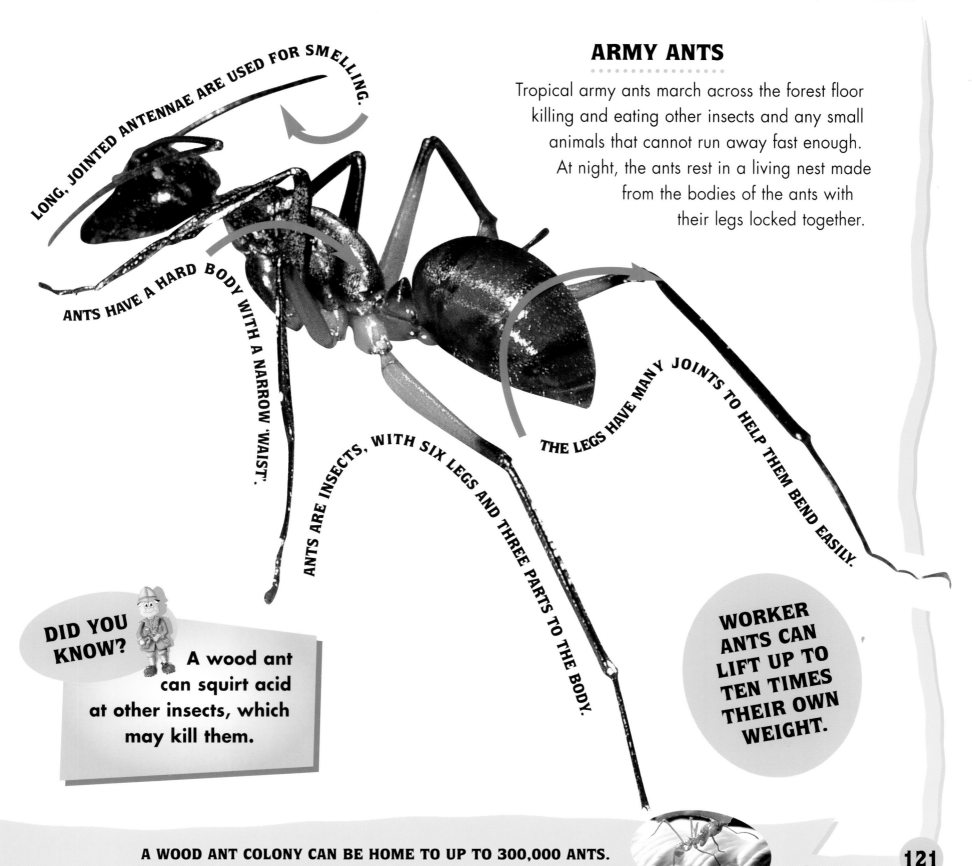

LONG, JOINTED ANTENNAE ARE USED FOR SMELLING.

ANTS HAVE A HARD BODY WITH A NARROW 'WAIST'.

ANTS ARE INSECTS, WITH SIX LEGS AND THREE PARTS TO THE BODY.

THE LEGS HAVE MANY JOINTS TO HELP THEM BEND EASILY.

DID YOU KNOW? A wood ant can squirt acid at other insects, which may kill them.

WORKER ANTS CAN LIFT UP TO TEN TIMES THEIR OWN WEIGHT.

A WOOD ANT COLONY CAN BE HOME TO UP TO 300,000 ANTS.

THE ANIMAL QUIZ

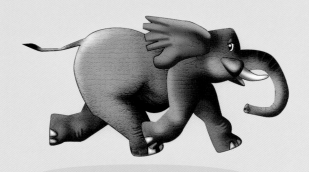

1. WHICH BABY PETS LOOK LIKE PINK JELLY BABY SWEETS?

a) hamsters
b) rabbits
c) guinea pigs

2. WHY DO DOGS WAG THEIR TAILS?

a) to keep cool
b) because they are happy or excited
c) to make them run faster

3. WHY DO PONIES WEAR HORSESHOES?

a) to protect their hooves and help them grip the ground
b) because they don't like getting their feet wet
c) it makes them taller so they can see over jumps

4. WHAT COLOUR ARE ALBINO GUINEA PIGS?

a) black and white striped
b) white with green spots
c) white with red eyes

5. WHY DO RABBITS THUMP THEIR BACK LEGS?

a) because they are hungry
b) to warn other rabbits of danger
c) because they are practising for sports day

6. HOW MANY EGGS DOES A FEMALE GOLDFISH LAY EACH YEAR?

a) about one million
b) about 10
c) about 100

7. WHY DO PET CATS OFTEN SCRATCH THE FURNITURE?

a) to sharpen their claws
b) to make you buy new furniture
c) because they want to go outside

8. WHICH FURRY ANIMAL LIKES TO HAVE STINK FIGHTS?

a) ring-tailed lemur
b) gorilla
c) lion

9. WHICH ANIMALS CAN FLY?

a) birds
b) bats
c) insects

10. WHY DO TREE FROGS HAVE STICKY FEET?

a) they have chewing gum on their toes
b) they have special 'glue' on their toes
c) they varnish their toenails

11. HOW LONG CAN AN ELEPHANT LIVE?

a) about 30 years
b) about 150 years
c) about 70 years

12. WHICH BIRD COULD BITE OFF A PERSON'S FINGER?

a) a macaw
b) a pigeon
c) a penguin

13. WHICH CAT CANNOT PURR?

a) pet cat
b) tiger
c) bobcat

14. WHY DOES A GORILLA HAVE A BIG HEAD?

a) he thinks he's the greatest
b) he eats a lot
c) he has a big brain

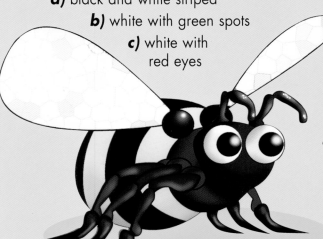

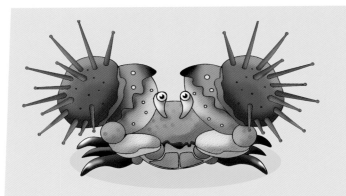

15. WHICH OCEAN ANIMAL LIKES TO PLAY WITH PEOPLE?
a) shark
b) crab
c) dolphin

16. WHICH SEAL HAS A NOSE LIKE AN ELEPHANT?
a) jumbo seal
b) trumpet seal
c) elephant seal

17. WHICH FISH LAYS ITS EGGS IN A MERMAID'S PURSE?
a) dogfish
b) rainbow fish
c) mermaid fish

18. HOW DO SALMON RECOGNISE THE RIVERS WHERE THEY WERE BORN?
a) by the colour of the water
b) by the smell of the water
c) by the name of the river

19. WHICH FISH HAS BOTH EYES ON THE SAME SIDE OF ITS HEAD?
a) a flatfish
b) a monocle fish
c) a cyclops fish

20. WHICH FISH HAS A POUCH LIKE A KANGAROO?
a) a female kangaroo fish
b) a male pouch fish
c) a male seahorse

21. WHAT DOES A BOXER CRAB WEAR ON ITS PINCERS?
a) boxing gloves
b) sea anemones
c) pincer shells

22. WHY DO SNOWY OWLS HAVE WHITE FEATHERS?
a) for camouflage against the snow
b) because they don't like bright colours
c) to make them show up in the dark

23. WHICH EAGLE BUILDS THE BIGGEST NEST IN THE WORLD?
a) the bald eagle
b) the stick eagle
c) the giant eagle

24. HOW BIG IS AN OSTRICH'S EGG?
a) as big as 4 chicken's eggs
b) as big as 24 chicken's eggs
c) as big as 20 chicken's eggs

25. WHICH BIRD IS GOOD AT TOBOGGANING?
a) the penguin
b) the snowy owl
c) the sledge gull

26. WHY DO FEMALE PEACOCKS HAVE DULL FEATHERS?
a) because they don't like showing off
b) because brown is their favourite colour
c) because they are camouflaged for sitting on their eggs

27. WHY DOES A SEAGULL HAVE WEBBED FEET?
a) for swimming
b) for making its nest
c) for fighting other seagulls

28. WHICH BABY BIRDS LIKE MILK?
a) milk owls
b) pigeons
c) cereal gulls

29. WHY DO SOME SHEEP HAVE FAT TAILS?
a) to store energy for when food is scarce
b) to make a soft cushion for sitting on
c) because they eat too much chocolate

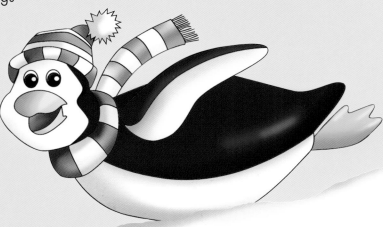

30. HOW MANY STOMACHS DOES A COW HAVE?

a) four

b) two small ones and six large ones

c) one with four chambers

31. WHY DOES A DOG HAVE A WET NOSE?

a) to help it pick up smells

b) because it doesn't have a handkerchief

c) to help it to keep cool

32. WHY DO ROOSTERS CROW 'COCK-A-DOODLE-DO'?

a) to wake everyone up in the morning

b) to show they are in charge

c) to practise their singing

33. HOW MANY PIGLETS CAN A SOW HAVE IN A YEAR?

a) about 22

b) about 2

c) about 12

34. WHICH ANIMAL IS STRONGER THAN A SHIRE HORSE?

a) a strongman

b) a leopard

c) an elephant

35. WHICH GOATS PRODUCE MOHAIR WOOL?

a) mohair goats

b) angora goats

c) woolly goats

36. WHICH IS THE LARGEST LIZARD IN THE WORLD?

a) Komodo dragon

b) giant gecko

c) dragon lizard

37. WHICH LIZARD WEARS GLASSES?

a) glass chameleon

b) gecko

c) four-eyed monitor lizard

38. WHICH REPTILE IS GOOD AT CHANGING COLOUR?

a) rainbow boa

b) paintbox turtle

c) chameleon

39. WHICH TORTOISE HAS A VERY FLAT SHELL?

a) pancake tortoise

b) squashed tortoise

c) paper tortoise

40. WHY DO BOAS HAVE HEAT HOLES ON THEIR LIPS?

a) to heat up their food

b) to sense the hot bodies of their prey

c) to keep their heads warm

41. WHICH LIZARD CAN WALK ON WATER?

a) basilisk lizard

b) miracle lizard

c) water-walker lizard

42. HOW OFTEN DO SNAKES SHED THEIR SKIN?

a) once in a lifetime

b) once every six years

c) up to six times a year

43. HOW MANY HOURS A DAY DO LIONS SPEND SLEEPING?

a) up to 20 hours

b) up to 5 hours

c) up to 12 hours

44. WHY DO WOLVES HOWL?

a) they didn't get what they wanted for Christmas

b) they are talking to other wolves

c) they are hungry

45. WHICH ANIMAL CAN WAIT TWO YEARS BETWEEN MEALS?
a) a big crocodile
b) a big lion
c) a big polar bear

46. WHICH MOSQUITOES BITE PEOPLE?
a) male mosquitoes
b) female mosquitoes
c) baby mosquitoes

47. WHERE IS A SCORPION'S STING?
a) on its pincers
b) on its left front leg
c) on its tail

48. WHICH POISONOUS FISH DO PEOPLE SOMETIMES EAT?
a) pufferfish
b) lionfish
c) snakefish

49. WHICH FAMOUS PERSON ARE TEDDY BEARS NAMED AFTER?
a) Ted Heath
b) Ted Roosevelt
c) Teddyboy Slim

50. WHICH BEETLES EAT POO?
a) smell beetles
b) poo beetles
c) dung beetles

51. WHICH INSECTS DRINK THROUGH A STRAW?
a) butterflies and moths
b) cockroaches
c) grasshoppers

52. WHICH MOTHS ARE LIKE JET PLANES?
a) jumbo jet moths
b) hawk moths
c) harrier moths

53. WHY DO EARTHWORMS HAVE A SLIMY SKIN?
a) because they use too much skin cream
b) to help them slide through the soil
c) to help their clothes slide on more easily

54. WHICH SPIDER IS AS BIG AS A DINNER PLATE?
a) Goliath tarantula
b) giant hunting spider
c) mega jumping spider

55. WHICH CREEPY CRAWLY HAS ONLY GOT ONE FOOT?
a) the foot ant
b) a snail
c) a beetle with three legs missing

56. WHICH ANTS GROW MUSHROOMS?
a) leafcutter ants
b) mushroom ants
c) gardener ants

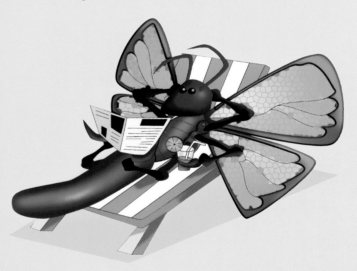

ANSWERS

1 a), 2 b), 3 a), 4 c), 5 b), 6 c), 7 a), 8 a), 9 a)b)c), 10 b), 11 c), 12 a), 13 b), 14 c), 15 c), 16 c), 17 a), 18 b), 19 a), 20 c), 21 b), 22 a), 23 a), 24 b), 25 a), 26 c), 27 a), 28 b), 29 a), 30 c), 31 a), 32 b), 33 a), 34 c), 35 b), 36 a), 37 b), 38 c), 39 a), 40 b), 41 a), 42 c), 43 c), 44 b), 45 a), 46 b), 47 c), 48 a), 49 b), 50 c), 51 a), 52 b), 53 b), 54 a), 55 b), 56 a).

INDEX